MEET
at the
ORANGE BLOSSOM

Night Lights
in
Buxton

Henry and Michal Schliff
Buxton, North Carolina 27920

Meet Me at the Orange Blossom
by Henry and Michal Schliff

ISBN: 0-9658965-0-1

About the Cover Artist

Cliff Morrow, a year-round Hatteras Island resident, is a graduate of the Art Institute of Pittsburgh and a former staff artist with the Carnegie Museum of Natural History, where he was Chairman of the Exhibits Department before his retirement in 1988.

Interior Drawings: By Michal

INTRODUCTION

Meet Me at the Orange Blossom

The salt-tang of the sea mingles with the aromas of fresh-baked sweets and just-cooked donuts as the daily regulars settle down at their corner round table in the tearoom with hot coffee, fluffy biscuits and crisp-chewy bagels. Surfers and wind-sailors, dripping with seawater and sun, burst indoors, bringing with them the vigor of wind and waves. Lean, tanned, muscular and fit, they order huge apple uglies and eat them where they stand, then come back for seconds, with the inevitable, "Don't bother with the bag, ma'am." Refueled with sugar and orange juice, the wind-sailors are off again to the nearby Canadian Hole, and the surfers head back to Lighthouse Beach, the premiere surfing spot, so they like to say, on the entire East Coast.

As they depart, the schoolkids arrive. The teenagers, sleepy-eyed and polite, pick up quick breakfast biscuits, sweet rolls, and cinnamon swirls, while the younger ones line up for melt-in-the-mouth chocolate satin donuts.

8:00 a.m. comes and goes. There is a breath of quiet, space and time for regulars to refill their coffee, and then the fishermen saunter in, in-between tides. They are solid, hearty men and earthy, plain-speaking women, and their eyes twinkle with the barely-contained secret that though they long for fish, they are content with or without a catch, for it is a good thing to be alive on this particular day, in this particular place.

They settle down on the porch with fish tales and sweets and watch the sightseers arrive, the ones who are eager to climb the Lighthouse and experience our island-jewel from a breathtakingly new perspective. The sightseers—couples, families, retired folk, professional people, foreign groups—drift into the tearoom and out onto the porch, mingling with the regulars and the fishermen, blending into the Orange Blossom day.

Thus the morning hours pass. Around 11:00 the pizza warmer is placed in the bakery case and fresh, hot deep-dish pizza pies are put on display. The locals—commercial fishermen, artists, carpenters, surf-board makers, shop owners, park rangers, deputies, and women fresh from yoga class—arrive early for their thick slice of pizza and a bowl of hot or cold homemade soup. They move into the tearoom and pull out any available chair. The conversation flows from table to table while people await their sandwiches and Mexican specialty orders. As an impossibly high sandwich is placed before a newcomer to Orange Blossom sandwiches, there is a round of good-natured laughter over the expression on the newcomer's face when he exclaims, "I'm supposed to eat the whole thing?!"

When the noon hour gives way to early afternoon, the locals depart and the tourists—temporarily freed from the demands of a workday schedule—drift in for a leisurely lunch. Their talk of the pleasures of the morning and the anticipated adventure of the afternoon oftentimes draws a friendly comment or suggestion from someone at a nearby table. Island experiences are exchanged. Introductions are made.

3

Throughout the day it happens—people meeting at The Orange Blossom, whether by chance or by prior arrangement. Geographically it is an easy place for islanders to come together and for tourists to gather, located as it is in the heart of "downtown" Buxton, near the famous Cape Hatteras Lighthouse and the popular windsurfers' mecca, The Canadian Hole. I use quotation marks around "downtown," because none of the island's villages is large enough for there to be such a thing as a real downtown, but here in Buxton the bakery is surrounded by the local bank, a frozen yogurt shop, gas stations, tackle shops, and a fine neighborhood market just down the way. It's as downtown as there is on Hatteras Island.

In the fifties there were orange trees on the Orange Blossom property. They were presumably planted by the Barnettes, who built the Orange Blossom Motel. Before the advent of the motel, the land was home to an abundance of live oaks, their roots sinking and spreading beneath the sandy soil of a high dune rise. It was in all likelihood a part of the ancient ground that was home to the Algonquin Indian nation who flourished before the time of Christ in the place which white settlers later referred to simply as the Cape, until the postal service changed the name to Buxton.

After Mr. Barnette's death, the motel was bought by Doris and Allan Oakham and Lillian Hundley. They converted the motel into a bakery. In 1991 my husband Henry Schliff and I took over the property from the Oakhams and made further conversions, keeping the bakery and establishing a restaurant.

Henry and I came to the island from Chapel Hill, North Carolina, where we had also been in the restaurant business as owner-operators of Papagayo Restaurant. For ten years before buying the Chapel Hill Papagayo, Henry was the Director of Operations of the Papagayo Mexican Restaurant chain. During those years, he developed the menu and recipes used in all the restaurants. His original chef's training was in French cooking. He was the first graduate of the chefs' training program run by noted French chef and cookbook author, Madeleine Kamman.

As you read through our cookbook, you will find that the recipes Henry has created for The Orange Blossom reflect his training in French cooking along with his long experience in working with Mexican ingredients.

We have included anecdotes and stories about the recipes and our years on Hatteras Island and in the cooking trade, for just as others meet at The Orange Blossom, we would like for you to meet us here, too. I am Henry's wife, the first-person writer of the stories and anecdotes in our book. My name is Michal. Henry and I have a son whose name is also Henry. He is a homeschool student, a talented martial-artist, an inventive cook who helps us daily in the bakery, and our joy.

As we meet you here in the doorway of The Orange Blossom, we would like to invite you to step inside and visit with us for awhile. Pull out a chair, prop up your feet, breathe in the salt air, relax, enjoy, while we offer you stories and refreshment, the gifts of our hearts to yours.

ACKNOWLEDGEMENTS

We wish to thank Doris and Allan Oakham and Lillian Hundley who introduced us to The Orange Blossom way and made our move to Buxton possible.

To Ruth Smith, Jeannie Cox, Mary O Morgan, and Doris Jennette, we would like to express our deepest appreciation for your support and your good humor in the face of crowds and kitchen chaos.

To Bill Smith—bless you for tearing down the deck and letting in the light.

To Honest Bill Crook—thanks for the hot peppers and for joining us on "another day in paradise."

To Shawn Stahlman and Jeremy Boyce—thanks for being with us as you grow. And to Shawn a special thanks for coming to work every day at 5:00 a.m., and doing it with a smile.

To our son Henry—our love and appreciation for all that you are and do.

To our customers and our Hatteras Island community—thank you for being here with us.

And to Irene Nolan and Tony McGowan of The Island Breeze, our grateful appreciation for providing us with a monthly forum for our stories and recipes.

MEET ME AT THE ORANGE BLOSSOM
Table of Contents

Morning Sweets, Treats and Breads

Soups

Sandwich Dressings and Spreads

Pizzas

Morning Sweets, Treats, and Breads

On an Orange Blossom
Morning

ON A BAKERY MORNING

The one who would eat only apple turnovers was tall and lean, dour of countenance and taciturn in manner. His companion was shorter and lacked the squared-off edges of the apple-turnover man. He had a round cherub-like face, rounded shoulders, and a belly that did not protrude too far but curved subtly toward convexity beneath the bib overalls he wore.

The round man was the spokesman for the two. I did not realize at first that he actually preferred cherry turnovers, for if we happened to have only the apple turnovers on hand, he took two of them for himself with a complaisant, accommodating air. It was the morning when we were left with only cherry turnovers in the Orange Blossom case that I discovered the truth of the matter.

"I'm sorry," I said when he approached the bakery case, with his taciturn friend trailing along in his wake, "We've got just the cherry turnovers left today."

"Well," he said, smiling in his pleasant way, "that's all right for me, but"—he paused and looked over his shoulder. "They've sold out of apple," he reported to his friend, then added sheepishly, in a lowered voice, as if he were somehow personally accountable for this state of affairs with the turnovers, "They've still got cherry."

The dour one stopped in his tracks and stared.

"No apple?" he said at last. This was directed to his friend. He did not once look at me.

"They're sold out," the round one repeated. "For today anyways." Turning back to me with a vaguely apologetic air, he said, "I'll take two cherry turnovers and a coffee."

The apple-turnover man headed to the coffee machine and pulled two cups from the receptacle. This was their routine. The apple-turnover man poured their coffees, and the round one ordered for both of them. They paid separately.

"You havin' anything?" the round one asked as his friend poured the coffee. *Anything*, I knew, included only turnovers. Neither man ate donuts, Danish, bars, biscuits, or bagels.

The taciturn one poured with concentration and did not speak until he was finished. "No," he said finally.

"Well then," the round one said, "I guess that'll be all. Just the two cherry turnovers and a coffee for me. I'll get his coffee today."

I rang up the sale while the taciturn one headed into the tearoom with the two coffees.

They had been in the bakery everyday for a week, arriving in the late morning, sometime between 11:30 and noon.

"Would you like to reserve four apple turnovers for tomorrow morning?" I asked as I counted out his change. "It's hard to tell how many of each kind to make everyday. If we know you want four apple turnovers, we'll be glad to save them for you."

"Oh, no," he said hastily, "I wouldn't go and do that. You know"—his sheepish grin appeared—"I actually prefer the cherry myself. But he don't like nothin' besides the apple."

"I could keep them for you—two apple and two cherry."

"Oh, no," he repeated. "If the flounder's bitin', we might not come in off the beach. No, we'll just see what you've got when we git here."

Nonetheless, I saved them—two apple and two cherry—every morning that October. And though the flounder were often biting, the two of them never failed to come in, regular as clockwork. They drove a pick-up truck, which they parked beneath the big oak tree. After they parked, they sat there in the truck for a few minutes. I always wondered why, and finally decided it was because they did not want to rush from one setting to another. They liked to ease themselves into a situation.

The taciturn one finally eased himself into talking with me on those quiet sun-drenched October mornings. The conversations were always brief. How were the flounder today?...Got a few pretty ones. How was the water?...Clear. I struggled to think of what to say about flounder, which I had decided was his passion. Did he eat the flounder he caught? This brought, at first, an uncomprehending stare, then a question in reply: "Who *don't* eat flounder?" That man or woman clearly wasn't worth thinking about, in my flounder fisherman's view.

And that was how I began to think of the two of them as the October days slipped by, one by leisurely one: my flounder fishermen. Regular, reliable, with a sense of order and a certainty in their preferences—men who savored their moments and their fish. We have had others like them in the bakery, women as well as men, after the frenetic rush of fun-seeking, taste-testing families gives way to the patient pace of the older ones, who have developed an appreciation for slow moments and flounder and the uncomplicated goodness of turnovers.

When the flounder were gone, so too were my flounder fishermen. They return every spring and fall when the flounder are biting. I keep the turnovers waiting.

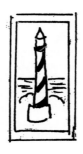

APPLE UGLIES

An especially popular item on our bakery menu is the apple ugly. In the summer lines stretch out the front door with people waiting to buy them fresh and hot. Tom Tuley, editor of the *Evansville Courier*, wrote in that newspaper that "as close to paradise as I have ever been is stopping by the Orange Blossom at 6 A.M. on a calm summer morning, walking to an empty beach with an apple ugly and a cup of coffee, and watching the dolphins play, with only the roar of the ocean and the wail of the gulls breaking the silence."

It is the bakery's signature item. As with most of what goes on at The Orange Blossom, the creation of the apple ugly was sheer serendipity. Before establishing the bakery in 1980, Doris and Allan Oakham owned a bakery in Virginia. There, donuts were only a small part of the business, but Doris and Allan soon discovered that the people on Hatteras Island had a nearly insatiable craving for deep-fried, raised donuts. So they were added to the bakery items at The Orange Blossom. As the popularity of the donuts grew by leaps and bounds, so too did the amount of donut scraps that had to be dealt with.

One day a retired baker from Kentucky named Preston Smith visited the bakery. As with many of The Orange Blossom customers, he made his way back to the kitchen to pass the time of day. Noticing a pile of donut scraps on the baker's table where Allan was cutting out donuts, he said, "Let me show you a good way to use those scraps." He proceeded to chop the dough, then he added apples and shaped the dough into pretty little pieces. After allowing the dough to rise, he fried it. The results were beautiful fritters.

After the Kentucky baker's departure, Allan and Doris decided to try to reproduce the beautiful fritters. Allan made up the dough, and Doris fried the fritters. No matter how hard she tried, she could not succeed in producing beautiful, or even pretty, fritters.

"Why," she exclaimed in disgust, "these are the ugliest things I ever saw!"

But they tasted delicious. When Doris put them in the bakery case, customers laughed at their looks, but they snatched them up and ate them as quickly as they could be made.

Mrs. Barbara J. Hehl, a long-time bakery customer, insists that she was actually the one who gave them their name. As she recounts the story, "I suggested since they had apples in the dough and when cooked they spread out in ugly shapes that they call them apple uglies so that is what they named them."

Many people claim to have named them, for the natural response of anyone seeing the misshapen things in the case is to exclaim, "Oooh, aren't they ugly!" The name stuck. People come from miles around to buy apple uglies. Tourists have made a tradition of buying dozens at a time to take back home to relatives in Ohio, Pennsylvania, New Jersey, Key West, and Quebec. In this way, The Orange Blossom has become known as "the home of the apple ugly."

The apple ugly is thus to the Orange Blossom as salt air is to the ocean. Though the following recipe which Henry has created for home use does not exactly duplicate the apple ugly at The Orange Blossom, it will give you, when you are hundreds of miles away, a taste of Hatteras.

Missing "secret ingredients": Hatteras Island air; Hatteras Island humidity; Orange Blossom tradition; Orange Blossom proof box with erratic temperature control; Baker's judgment to know the exact moment to cook them; Baker's knowledge of how to transfer uglies from pan to hot oil without deflating the risen dough; Baker's judgment to know the exact moment they are done; A perfect summer day; The grace of God.

APPLE UGLIES

1 package dry yeast
½ cup warm water (110 degrees)
½ cup warm evaporated milk (110 degrees)
6 tablespoons granulated sugar
¼ cup shortening

1 large egg, beaten
1 teaspoon vanilla
3½ cups all-purpose flour
1 teaspoon salt
¼ teaspoon mace or nutmeg
1 cup chopped apple pie filling
¾ teaspoon cinnamon

Whisk the yeast into the warm water. In an electric mixer, cream the sugar and shortening. Add the egg, vanilla, milk and yeast. Mix together the flour, salt, and mace and stir into the liquid ingredients. Beat for 8 minutes (or knead by hand on a lightly floured surface). Place dough in a lightly oiled bowl, cover, and let rise until double. Remove dough from bowl and place on a lightly floured board. Roll into a sheet about ½ inch thick. Spread apple filling evenly over the top and sprinkle with cinnamon. Using a dough scraper, chop the dough into pieces vertically and then horizontally. Using ½ cup of chopped dough at a time, mold into oblong, irregular shapes and place 2 inches apart on a large baking pan. Cover with another pan, leaving room for dough to rise. Let rise until double in volume. In a deep skillet heat vegetable shortening to 375 degrees. Dip a metal pancake turner into the hot fat, carefully slide it under the risen dough and place uglies into skillet a few at a time (do not crowd). Cook for about 1½ minutes until golden brown underneath, turn, and continue cooking for 1½ minutes. Using tongs place cooked uglies on a metal rack to drain. Drizzle with icing (recipe on next page).

(Continued on next page)

(Apple Uglies, continued)

Icing

4 cups powdered sugar   **6 tablespoons water**

Mix together.

STICKY BUNS

Sticky buns disappear from our bakery case quickly in the morning and are best eaten fresh from the oven.

Sweet Dough

2 tablespoons dry yeast   **½ cup vegetable shortening**
½ cup warm milk (110 degrees) **2 large eggs**
½ cup warm water (110   **¼ teaspoon lemon extract**
**   degrees)**   **4¼ cups all-purpose flour**
½ cup sugar   **1 teaspoon salt**

Combine milk and water and stir in yeast. In the bowl of an electric mixer cream the sugar and shortening. Beat in the eggs one at a time. Pour in the yeast mixture and lemon extract. Combine the flour and salt and add to mixing bowl. Beat with a dough hook for 8 minutes until dough is soft and supple (or stir together and knead by hand on a lightly floured surface). Place dough in a lightly oiled bowl, cover and let rise until double in volume (about 2 hours).

Smear

½ cup granulated sugar   **1 tablespoon plus 2**
½ cup brown sugar   **   teaspoons flour**
½ cup vegetable shortening   **½ teaspoon salt**
                                    ½ cup light corn syrup

In the bowl of an electric mixer, combine the sugars, shortening, flour and salt. Beat 5 minutes on medium speed until mixture is very light and fluffy. Continue beating and add the corn syrup in a slow steady stream.

Final Assembly and Baking

vegetable oil   **¼ cup raisins**
2 tablespoons sugar mixed   **¾ cup chopped pecans**
**   with ½ teaspoon cinnamon**

(Continued on next page)

(Sticky Buns, continued)

On a lightly floured surface, roll the dough into a rectangle about ¼ inch thick. Lightly brush with vegetable oil. Leaving a strip 2 inches from the bottom, sprinkle cinnamon and sugar evenly over the rest of the dough. Evenly distribute raisins over the sugar and roll the dough into a cylinder by starting at the top and rolling down to the bottom, sealing edge with the heel of the hand. Cut cylinder into 7 equal pieces. Grease a 9 inch cake pan and cover bottom with a ¼ inch layer of smear. Sprinkle over pecans. Place 1 piece of dough flat side down in the middle of the pan and distribute the other pieces evenly around the center piece, leaving room for expansion of the dough. Cover and let rise in a warm place until double in volume. Bake in a 375 degree oven until the top is golden brown and glaze is lightly caramelized (use a spatula to lift the dough and peek underneath). Remove from oven and place a large serving plate face side down over the top of the pan and invert quickly to unmold (be very careful since glaze is very hot). Cool 5 minutes and serve.

CINNAMON ROLLS

sweet dough (see previous recipe under sticky buns)	⅓ cup raisins
	⅓ cup chopped pecans
2 tablespoons sugar mixed with ½ teaspoon cinnamon	½ teaspoon cinnamon
	2 tablespoons melted butter

On a lightly floured surface, roll the dough into a rectangle about ¼ inch thick. Lightly brush the top with melted butter. Leaving a strip 2 inches from the bottom, sprinkle the cinnamon and sugar mixture over the dough. Evenly distribute the raisins and pecans over the sugar. Sprinkle the additional ½ teaspoon of cinnamon over all. Form the dough into a cylinder by starting at the top and rolling down to the bottom, sealing the edge with the heel of the hand. Cut the cylinder into 7 equal pieces. Grease a 9 inch cake pan and place one piece of dough in the middle of the pan. Distribute the other pieces evenly around the center piece, leaving room for expansion of the dough. Cover and let rise in a warm place until double in volume. Bake in 375 degree oven until lightly browned on the bottom (be careful to not over-bake). Cool on a wire rack for five minutes. Remove from pan and return to wire rack. Spread icing over the top (recipe on next page).

(Continued on next page)

(Cinnamon Rolls, Continued)

Confectioner's Sugar Icing
2 cups confectioner's sugar   2 tablespoons water

Mix together to obtain a thick spreading consistency (adding a little more water if too thick).

CRANBERRY-ORANGE BLOSSOM MUFFINS

Bright, autumnal fruit, the cranberry contributes visual pleasure and tart taste to our Thanksgiving feasts and our Christmas tables. Throughout November and December we find cranberries fresh and whole in handy-sized plastic bags on our produce aisles or pureed into canned sauces arranged in prominent middle-of-the-aisle displays alongside the canned pumpkin, packaged stuffing mix, and instant mashed potato boxes.

When the holiday season ends, so too the prominence of the cranberry declines. The cans of sauce are returned to an obscure position on a grocery shelf and the plastic bags are tucked into a corner of the frozen food section to wait out another ten months of consumer apathy, regardless of the fact that the cranberry is one of those fruits that freezes exceedingly well and is therefore readily available for year-round use.

Like most people, I tend to compartmentalize the cranberry. It goes with a particular season, is a part of a traditional holiday menu. It wouldn't occur to me, for example, to eat cranberries in July.

Yesterday while Henry and Jeannie were cooking cranberries in our bakery kitchen, using them in breads, muffins, pudding and pies, I began to think—as the fresh, homely aromas of fruit and vanilla and baking bread drifted through the air—about the way we often compartmentalize not only seasonal fruits but also various aspects of our lives, placing them in neat closed-lid containers so that the contents do not spill over into other areas. As my thoughts turned down this path, an image leaped in front of me and I couldn't help laughing aloud, remembering Rachel.

She was a lawyer, a wife, a mother, and a karate student. She preferred to keep these areas of her life separate and distinct. With her fellow karate students, for example, she never discussed the law or the fact that she had a husband and son. I worked with her several evenings a week over a two-year period without knowing anything about her other than the fact that when she was annoyed she blinked, when she was intimidated, her chin quivered, when she was nervous her hands clenched and unclenched, when she was uncertain her shoulders lifted nearly to her ears. She was not a pretty woman; in fact, she was decidedly plain, with facial features that did not blend smoothly, a pallid complexion, and thin mouse-brown hair which she wore in a mannish cut. To and from class she wore unadorned but clean and pressed blue jeans, a long-sleeved, button-down collar shirt, and polished penny-loafers.

After we had been in karate class together for about two years, Rachel figuratively floored me one day by issuing an invitation. "I've got a tape of BLOODSPORT," she said. "It has some interesting fighting scenes. Would you like to come over and watch it with me?"

Bloodsport. Bloodsport. I wracked my brain. I wasn't up on martial art movies. In fact, I had never seen a single one and felt moderately certain that I didn't want to start now.

"It's the new Jean Claude Van Damme movie," she helpfully supplied. "Some of the techniques are outrageous and impractical, but still—" she shrugged—"there are some things one might learn from it."

"Well," I stuttered, "sure. Of course. That sounds…great!"

She gave me directions to her house. We set a time—an afternoon when she was off from work, but when her husband and son would not be home to distract us from the business of martial-arts watching.

Her house was a large-a very large—two-story colonial structure in a upscale suburban neighborhood. As instructed, I came to the side door. Rachel showed me in through an immaculate hallway off the kitchen. I had to duck past an enormous water-filled kicking bag she had set up in the doorway. Glancing into the kitchen as we passed, I noted that it was neat and sparkling clean. It was a house where one could literally eat off the floor. There were a lot of hallways in her house. We wound our way through them until we landed at the doorway of a cavernous den.

"Here we are," Rachel said.

I stood in the open double-door entry, my jaw hanging. "Yes," I finally managed to say, pasting a smile on my face in an attempt to cover my utter shock at this first glimpse of the contents of Rachel's den. "Yes, yes, here we are," I repeated brightly.

"Have a seat," Rachel said. "I've got the tape ready. Would you like tea?"

I took a hesitant step inside, then, unable to keep up any pretense, burst out, "My God, would you look at all these dolls!"

They were everywhere, easily a hundred of them. There were delicate, priceless china dolls perched on stands in glass-fronted cases, there were fat cuddly dolls seated in miniature rockers by the fire, dolls lounging on couches, life-sized, life-like dolls standing in corners. Any little girl who loved dolls would quite naturally suppose, upon entering Rachel's den, that she had cheated and got to Heaven without ever dying.

"I collect dolls," Rachel said, surveying her room, "as you've probably gathered." She seated herself on the couch next to a two-faced Tutti-Frutti doll. "Do you like dolls?"

"Why, yes, I do. Actually, I love dolls."

"Feel free to look around," she said, smiling slightly.

As I went about the room exclaiming over Rachel's dolls, she informed me that she had more dolls throughout the house. We took a tour. I saw her entire collection, heard stories about how she had acquired them. By the time we sat down on her couch in the den to watch BLOODSPORT, I was looking at Rachel through different eyes. While we sipped hot spiced tea from flowered mugs, Rachel, seated on my right, made frequent comments, waxing enthusiastic over various gruesome and vicious techniques. On my left sat a fat baby doll with bright blue eyes, a blue gingham dress, and a perpetually pleased expression on her face.

The best way I can think of now to describe that afternoon is to say that it was like eating cranberries in July. It was pouring life out of its compartments and mixing it all together. It was great fun.

In the bakery kitchen I told Jeannie the story of Rachel's dolls. "It just goes to show how little we really know about people," she said. "There's so much we would never guess."

"But it doesn't have anything to do with cranberries," Henry noted as he pulled a pan of cranberry-orange blossoms from the oven.

"It has to do with compartments," I said.

He sighed. "I'm going to type out cranberry recipes," he said.

Though it is now cranberry season as I write, I hope you'll make our cranberry-orange blossom muffins in other seasons of the year, and as you bite into a fluffy, juice-bursting morsel, I wish you great fun - summer, spring, winter and fall.

CRANBERRY-ORANGE BLOSSOM MUFFINS

Beautiful to behold when baked.

1½ sticks butter, softened
1⅓ cups sugar
4 large eggs
4 cups flour
4 teaspoons baking powder
1 teaspoon salt

2 teaspoons grated orange
   rind
1⅓ cups milk
½ teaspoon orange extract
2 cups fresh cranberries
⅔ cup chopped pecans

In an electric mixer, cream the butter and sugar. Beat in the eggs one at a time. Combine the flour, baking powder, salt and orange rind. Beat the flour mixture and milk alternately into the creamed mixture. Add the orange extract and fold into the cranberries and pecans. Scoop into 12 well greased muffin cups and bake in a 350 degree oven until an inserted toothpick comes out clean. Cool on a wire rack for a few minutes and remove muffins from pan. Spread tops with orange icing.

Orange Icing
1¾ cups powdered sugar
2 tablespoons orange juice

2 tablespoons orange
   marmalade

Heat the marmalade briefly to liquefy. Place sugar in the bowl of an electric mixer and beat in the orange juice and marmalade to obtain a spreading consistency.

BRAN MUFFINS

3 cups All Bran cereal
1 cup raisins
¼ cup molasses
1 cup boiling water
¼ cup vegetable oil
¼ cup applesauce
2 eggs, beaten

2 cups buttermilk
2½ cups all-purpose flour
1 teaspoon cinnamon
2 tablespoons sugar
1 teaspoon baking soda
2 teaspoons baking powder
½ teaspoon salt

Combine the cereal, raisins, and molasses in a bowl and stir in the boiling water. Stir in the oil and applesauce. Beat together the eggs and buttermilk and stir in. Mix together the remaining ingredients and stir in. Grease 18 muffin cups and fill ¾ full with batter. Bake in a 400 degree oven for 25 minutes. Remove from oven and let stand for 5 minutes. Unmold and cool on a wire rack.

ZUCCHINI DREAMS

3 cups all-purpose flour
¼ cup wheat germ
2 teaspoons baking soda
1 teaspoon salt
1½ teaspoons cinnamon
1 teaspoon nutmeg
4 large eggs

¾ cup brown sugar
¾ cup white sugar
1 cup vegetable oil
3 cups grated zucchini
1 cup raisins
1 cup pecan pieces

Grease 24 muffin cups. Mix together the flour, wheat germ, baking soda, salt, cinnamon, and nutmeg. In an electric mixer beat together the eggs, sugars, and oil until light and smooth. Beat in the zucchini. Beat in the dry ingredients and then the raisins and pecans. Fill the muffin cups ¾ full and bake in a 375 degree oven until a toothpick inserted in the center comes out clean. Cool for a few minutes and unmold onto a wire rack.

Glaze

2 tablespoons melted butter
2 cups powdered sugar

pineapple juice

In an electric mixer, beat together the butter and powdered sugar. Beat in enough pineapple juice to make a spreadable glaze. Spread the glaze over the cooled muffins.

BLUEBERRY MUFFINS

1½ sticks butter, softened	**4 teaspoons baking powder**
1⅓ cups sugar	**1 teaspoon salt**
4 large eggs	**1⅓ cups milk**
4 cups flour	**2 cups fresh blueberries**

In an electric mixer, cream the butter and sugar. Beat in the eggs one at a time. Combine the flour, baking powder, and salt. Beat the flour mixture and milk alternately into the creamed mixture. Fold in the blueberries. Scoop into 12 well greased muffin cups and bake in a 350 degree oven until an inserted toothpick comes out clean.

BUTTERMILK BISCUITS

What better way to awaken to the day than by breaking open a hot, steaming biscuit? I love biscuits with savory fillings and biscuits with sweet fillings. Since I can never decide which I like better, I do the sensible thing and eat them both ways. I even like them plain.

My Aunt Helen made the best plain biscuits I've ever tasted. My family used to visit her and Uncle Paul every Sunday afternoon when I was a child. They lived on a farm at the end of a long and rutted dirt road. The first thing I did upon my arrival was visit the barn. It was dark and quiet and smelled of hay and animals. After walking through the barn, I would go outdoors and climb onto the fence where there was a big "saltlick" for the cows. For some reason this saltlick fascinated me. I would look to right and left to make certain no one was watching besides the cows, and then I would taste the saltlick. It was always the same: salty. Afterwards I would clamber back over the fence and head for the backyard, where I liked to inspect the water-pump. The pump, too, was always the same.

I then proceeded into the kitchen, which, on a Sunday afternoon after a big Sunday dinner, was neat and scrubbed-looking. At one end of the kitchen was a pantry. Every Sunday I would open the door—knowing exactly what I would find: a bowlful of Sunday dinner biscuits waiting on a shelf within my reach. I always took two and ate them there in the pantry as I made a study of jars of pickle relish and home-canned tomatoes. I suspect now that Aunt Helen baked extra biscuits, knowing that I would be coming; but then, even though I knew they would be there in their bowl, there was still the element of suspense: would they be there *this* time? They always were.

Though the following biscuits are not Aunt Helen's, they are exceptionally good, whether served with a filling, or plain.

BUTTERMILK BISCUITS

3 cups self-rising Martha
    White Biscuit Flour
¾ teaspoon salt
½ teaspoon baking soda
¼ cup shortening

¼ cup butter, cut into pieces
1 egg, beaten
1 cup plus 2 tablespoons
    buttermilk

In a large mixing bowl, combine flour, salt and soda. Cut in shortening and butter. Combine egg and buttermilk and stir into flour and shortening mixture. Place dough on floured board and knead briefly. Pat or roll dough into a circle ½ inch high and cut into rounds with a biscuit cutter. Gather together dough scraps and repeat process. Place rounds, side by side, on a lightly greased sheet pan and bake in 425 degree oven till lightly browned (about 15 minutes).

LETHA'S ANGEL FLAKE BISCUITS

2 packages dry yeast
3 tablespoons warm water
5 cups soft white flour
4 tablespoons sugar
1 teaspoon baking powder

1½ teaspoons salt
1 teaspoon baking soda
1 cup shortening
2 cups buttermilk

Dissolve yeast in warm water. In a large mixing bowl sift together flour, sugar, baking powder, salt, and soda. Cut in the shortening and then stir in the yeast mixture and buttermilk. When dough comes together turn out onto floured surface and knead briefly. Place in lightly greased bowl, cover with plastic wrap and then a kitchen towel and let rise for one hour. On a floured surface, pat dough into a circle ½ inch high. Cut into rounds with a biscuit cutter and place side by side on a greased sheet pan. Cover loosely with plastic wrap or a light-weight towel and let rise double in a warm place. Bake in a 400 degree oven until lightly browned.

PERSEVERANCE COFFEE CAKE

About once a year it strikes me: the urge to try my hand once again at baking a coffee cake. Coffee cakes are not my forte. I have these ideas about what should go into them, including blueberries, buttermilk, sour cream, apples, pecans, lemon rind, cinnamon and allspice, brown sugar, lots of eggs. Obviously, one lone coffee cake cannot accommodate all of my desires. This year when the urge struck, I decided to approach the matter sensibly. I would refrain from putting all my eggs, so to speak, in one basket. I would bake at least two cakes, one with buttermilk, apples, and spices, and another with blueberries, lemon, and sour cream. Mentally I prepared my recipes, writing out all of my ingredients, even jotting down exact quantities, which is something I can rarely force myself to do. Since I had exactly enough buttermilk, apple, and eggs on hand to do the buttermilk cake, I began with it. I went through the recipe I had written, measuring carefully, doing everything neatly, even cleaning as I proceeded. Feeling extremely pleased with myself, I spread the batter in the pan and sprinkled my streusel topping over all. One lone pecan, dusted with sugar, butter, and cinnamon, fell onto the counter. I had been uncharacteristically careful during my preparations to refrain from tasting any stray tidbits, but here at the end I could not resist this one pecan piece. I popped it in my mouth, prepared to savor the sugary taste. Before my conscious mind could catch up with what was happening, I found myself staring at the pecan piece, lying once again on the counter where I had just spit it out, accompanied by a loud exclamation that was still ringing in my ears: "Ugghh!!" My mind stubbornly refusing to acknowledge what my taste buds already knew, I gingerly picked up the pecan piece between forefinger and thumb and sniffed, then licked. This time I threw the tidbit down in disgust and stomped my foot on the floor. "I don't believe this," I said aloud, glaring at the pan of batter. Feeling compelled to put the matter to rest, I stuck my forefinger down in the batter, then licked it. Salt. I had added ¾ cup of salt to my carefully thought-out coffee cake batter. There was nothing for it but to scrape the batter into the garbage can. I seriously considered giving up for another year, but as I reflected upon the matter, I realized that the recipe was sound; it was my lack of labeling that was to blame. After first removing the plastic container of salt from the counter and making a trip to the store to buy additional ingredients, I tried the cake again. It turned out well, so I called it Perseverance.

PERSEVERANCE COFFEE CAKE

2¼ cups flour
¼ teaspoon salt
1½ teaspoons cinnamon
¼ teaspoon ginger
¼ teaspoon allspice
¾ cup brown sugar
¾ cup white sugar

¾ cup butter
1 cup chopped pecans
1 teaspoon baking powder
1 teaspoon baking soda
1 egg
½ cup grated apple
¾ cup buttermilk

Grease a 9 x 12 inch baking pan and preheat oven to 350 degrees. Blend flour, a teaspoon of the cinnamon, remaining spices, and sugars. With a pastry blender cut in the butter until the mixture forms a crumbly meal. Remove ¾ cup of the mixture, toss with the pecans and ½ teaspoon cinnamon, and reserve for the topping. To the flour mixture add baking powder and soda and stir. In a separate bowl beat egg and add buttermilk and grated apple. Combine thoroughly, then stir into flour mix. Spread batter in baking pan, sprinkle topping over all, and bake for 30 to 35 minutes.

BLUEBERRY SOUR CREAM COFFEE CAKE

This coffee cake is light, fluffy, lovely to look at, and wonderful to taste morning, afternoon, or night. Depending on the season of the year, fresh raspberries or blackberries may be substituted for the blueberries with delicious results.

½ cup butter, softened
1 cup sugar
grated rind of 1 lemon
1 teaspoon lemon juice
1 teaspoon vanilla
2 eggs
1¾ cups flour

2 teaspoons baking powder
1 teaspoon baking soda
¼ teaspoon salt
1 cup sour cream
1 cup fresh blueberries
1 teaspoon flour

Topping
3 tablespoons flour
3 tablespoons butter,
    softened

½ cup sugar
½ cup chopped pecans

Grease a 9 x 12 inch baking pan and preheat oven to 350 degrees. In a mixer cream butter and sugar. Add grated lemon rind, lemon juice, and vanilla and beat. Add eggs one at a time and beat well. In a separate bowl blend flour, baking powder, baking soda, and salt. Add half of flour mixture to creamed mix and beat well. Add the sour cream, beating well, and then the remaining flour and blend. Rinse blueberries, drain, and toss with teaspoon of flour, then fold into the mix. Spread batter into the greased pan. To make topping, combine flour, sugar, and butter, cut into pieces, in mixing bowl. Beat with a paddle until the mixture is crumbly. Stir in pecans and spread topping over the batter. Bake for about 35 minutes.

TURKISH CUSTOMS APPLE COFFEE CAKE

My stepmother Letha was a cakebaker herself. All through the years of my adolescence and on into my adulthood, she baked cakes for me. When I was in college, she sent along cakes for my friends and me to enjoy during late-night talk sessions in our dorm room. When I was in airline stewardess school seven-hundred miles from home, she personally delivered a cake. When I was a receptionist in a New York City advertising agency, she mailed cakes to me and my roommate, Kay.

Perhaps her all-time-greatest cake sending occurred when I was a Peace Corps volunteer in Turkey and she mailed me one of the apple cakes she knew I loved. She baked it in a 9 x 13 inch aluminum pan that came with a slide-on lid. After cooling the cake on a rack, she reinserted it in the pan, slid on the lid and wrapped the whole thing securely in brown-paper packaging, tied it with twine and shipped it first-class mail from North Carolina to Izmir, Turkey.

A month later I received word from the postal service that I was to pick up a package at the customs office down at the Izmir docks. The Turkish customs clerks were deeply suspicious of Letha's apple cake. It had been sitting on their shelf for a good three weeks while they tried to ascertain if it contained subversive, illegal, or unsavory material. When they handed it over to me, the wrapping was torn, the twine was undone, and the cake was missing a corner. I didn't know whether to laugh or cry.

When I broke off a hunk of the cake and found that it was a little dry, but still wonderfully reminiscent of home, I did a little of both.

TURKISH CUSTOMS APPLE COFFEE CAKE

1 cup packed brown sugar
1 cup granulated sugar
3 eggs, beaten
1 teaspoon vanilla
1 teaspoon grated lemon
    rind
1 teaspoon lemon juice
1½ cups vegetable oil

3 cups flour
1 teaspoon baking soda
1½ teaspoons cinnamon
1 teaspoon nutmeg
1 teaspoon salt
3 cups grated apples
1 cup raisins
1 cup chopped pecans

Grease a 13 x 9 inch baking pan and line with wax paper. In a large bowl, stir together the sugars, eggs, vanilla, lemon rind, lemon juice, and oil. Combine the flour, baking soda, cinnamon, nutmeg and salt and add to bowl mixing well. Fold in the apples, raisins and pecans. Pour batter into prepared pan and bake in a 350 degree oven until a toothpick comes out clean when inserted in the center (about 50 minutes). Cool 5 minutes and invert onto a wire rack. Peel off paper and cool completely.

ORANGE BLOSSOM BANANA NUT BREAD

This recipe is a homestyle version of a bread made by Allan Oakham, the previous owner of our bakery, a wonderful man and a "baker from the old school" who knows all about simple pleasures and pure tastes.

2 packed cups of very ripe
    bananas
1 stick of butter, room
    temperature (must be
    very soft)
1½ cups sugar

4 eggs
2 tablespoons water
3 cups flour
1 tablespoon baking powder
1 teaspoon baking soda
½ cup chopped pecans

Combine the flour, baking powder, and soda. Set aside. Place the bananas in a mixing bowl and beat in the sugar and then the butter. Add the eggs and stir only until combined. Stir in the water. Add the flour mixture and pecans. Do not overbeat. Divide the mixture evenly between 2 medium sized, greased loaf pans. Place in a 325 degree oven and bake 35-45 minutes or until a toothpick inserted in the center comes out mostly clean. Cool for 5 minutes. Remove from pans and cool completely on a wire rack.

MORAVIAN COFFEE CAKE

1½ cups peeled and diced
   potatoes
1 cup water
1 package dry yeast
6 tablespoons butter
½ cup granulated sugar

½ teaspoon salt
1 egg, beaten
4 cups all-purpose flour
½ cup brown sugar
2 teaspoons cinnamon
2 tablespoons melted butter

Place potatoes in a saucepan, add 1 cup of water and bring to the boil. Cover and simmer over low heat until potatoes are tender. Drain, reserving the potato water. Puree the hot potatoes in an electric mixer. Beat in 6 tablespoons of butter, granulated sugar, salt, and ½ cup of potato water. Cool ¼ cup of potato water (adding tap water if there is not enough left) to 110 degrees and stir in the yeast. When potato mixture has cooled (110 degrees), beat in the yeast mixture. Beat in the egg and then the flour one cup at a time. Knead until dough is smooth and elastic (it will still be somewhat sticky). Place dough in a large, lightly oiled bowl. Cover with plastic wrap and then a kitchen towel. Let rise in a warm place until triple in volume. Press dough into a buttered 12 x 8½ x 2 inch baking pan. Combine brown sugar and cinnamon and sprinkle evenly over dough. Drizzle with melted butter. Cover pan with plastic wrap and let rise in a warm place until double in volume. Bake in a 350 degree oven for about 35 minutes (toothpick inserted in center will come out clean). Cool in pan for 10 minutes. Remove from pan. Cool 5 minutes more, cut into squares, and serve warm.

ITALIAN BREAD PUDDING

In the bakery we slice our homemade Italian bread by hand for making our lunch sandwiches—which means that we end up with a lot of leftover crusts. Since most people on our staff sensibly think that crusts are the best part of the bread, a certain portion of the leftovers get used up, but even a dedicated staff can consume only so many bread ends in a day's time. The crusts when cubed make excellent croutons for salads and soups (see croutons recipe, page 70). But still this doesn't account for all the leftovers. Part of the bread cubes are therefore used in making our wonderful sweet breakfast pudding, and another part in our homemade garlic croutons. Both are so good that it is well worth making homemade Italian bread for the sole purpose of cooking up a pudding or making croutons. It's okay to use store bought bread, but, as with most things culinary and otherwise, the finer the ingredients, the more splendid the results.

6 cups of Italian Bread cubes	**4 beaten eggs**
½ cup raisins	**¾ stick melted butter**
4 cups milk	**1 tablespoon vanilla**
	1¾ cups sugar

Place the bread cubes in a greased 9 x 13 x 2 inch baking pan. Sprinkle in the raisins. Mix together the eggs, milk, butter, and vanilla and pour over. Push any unsoaked bread pieces gently with your fingertips to completely immerse in the liquid. Let mixture rest for ten minutes and then bake in a 375 degree oven until the custard is set and the top is lightly browned (about 50 minutes). Cut into squares and serve with warm vanilla custard (see recipe page 32).

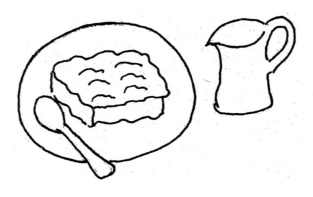

RICE PUDDING

Vanilla Custard
2 cups milk
2 cups half-and-half
4 large eggs
1 cup sugar
¼ cup cornstarch

2 teaspoons pure vanilla
   extract
1 can sweetened condensed
   milk

Scald the milk and half-and-half. Mix together the sugar and cornstarch. In an electric mixer, beat the eggs well. Continue beating while gradually adding the sugar and cornstarch. Slowly beat in the hot milk and half-and-half. Pour into a heavy-bottomed pot and cook over moderate heat, stirring constantly to 180 degrees (custard will thicken). Pour into a bowl and stir in the vanilla and condensed milk.

Pudding
1½ cups cooked plain rice   3 cups vanilla custard

In a bowl combine the rice with 3 cups of the hot custard (reserving the rest). Pour rice mixture into an 8 inch square cake pan and bake in a 350 degree oven until set (about 25 minutes). Cool completely. Serve in deep bowls, spooning some of the reserved custard over the top.

ARBORIO RICE CUSTARD

1 cup Arborio rice
2½ cups water
1 tablespoon butter
1 tablespoon vanilla
2 teaspoons fresh lime juice

1 can sweetened condensed
   milk
2 tablespoons sugar
2 eggs
2 cups whole milk

Rinse rice in a colander. Bring water to boil in a heavy-bottomed saucepan. Add the rice, butter, vanilla, and lime juice. Stir, then reduce heat to low, cover, and simmer for 20 minutes. Turn off heat. Add sweetened condensed milk and sugar and stir. In a separate bowl beat the eggs until frothy and blend in the milk. Stir the egg mixture into the rice and stir over medium heat for about 5 minutes, or until the mixture begins to bubble. Transfer to an oven-proof buttered casserole dish and bake in a 325 degree oven for 15 minutes, or until the custard is just set.

Soups

We're busy cooking
on our single burner stove.

ON THE WAY TO MARMARIS

We had been living in Turkey for several months, the two of us working in our separate Peace Corps sites. My job was in Buca, not far from Izmir. Henry lived about a two-and-a-half hour's bus ride north of me, in a picturesque Aegean village called Ayvalik. We decided to take a holiday trip together. Neither of us now can remember what the holiday was, and neither of us can remember the name of the town where we stopped to spend the night on our way south to the jewel-like town of Marmaris. We traveled by bus, and we stayed in a rather prosperous hotel in whatever the town was. The weather was cold and clear. We dined in the hotel dining room and went to bed in the unheated room with blankets piled high. Our thoughts, the next morning when we awoke early to catch the dawn bus, were of Marmaris, where we knew we would find balmy weather and a radiant blue sea. The hotel dining room was not yet open. We set out to find something to eat. An early-morning fog, chilly and damp, wrapped the streets in its thick cloak. No one was about. No lights were on in any of the buildings we passed. We were about to give up and turn back when ahead we noticed the gray nondescript shapes of Turkish men entering a shop door. Bright yellow light, fuzzy around the edges, poured out of the windows. It was a Turkish soup shop.

We entered to find the small room overflowing with men sitting at plain wooden tables, hunched over their bowls of soup, most of them eating with quiet concentration, others talking with an air of absentmindedness, not really wanting to be distracted from the serious morning business of filling their bellies with the thick, steaming bright green soup called mercimek corba.

Henry and I found a place at a counter. Two huge wide bowls of soup were placed before us. I inhaled the steam, picked up a slice of lemon set on the side of the plate, and squeezed it into the soup, then stirred the lemon and the layer of virgin olive oil floating on top into the body of the soup. The Turkish lentil (mercimek) was a lighter green than any lentil I've found in this country. It produced a soup that came closer to being the color of split pea soup, but it tasted infinitely better. And it had a clean, fresh smell that was entirely unlike the rather unpleasant, heavy scent of split peas.

As we ate our soup, we broke off hunks of the coarse, hearty Turkish bread and dunked them into the broth as everyone around us was doing. There were also black olives and a chunk of strong white goat milk cheese similar to feta. And, of course, strong hot tea served in little glass carafes.

When we had eaten our fill, we sat for a few moments enjoying the warmth in our stomachs and the heat of the room, a heat created by so many people pressed into the small space and by the huge pots of soup simmering on the stove behind the counter where we sat. In too brief a time, we had to leave. We didn't want to miss the Marmaris bus and be left behind in this small town, the name of which we didn't even know. But as we emerged from the warmth of the Turkish soup kitchen into the first light of a crisp early-winter day, I glanced back into the window and knew that wherever I traveled, I would never forget the experience of going out before dawn in an unknown town and finding perfect sustenance and complete comfort amongst strangers. But my attention was quickly drawn from the window and out to the sunlight burning off the fog and making visible all the bustle and business attendant upon the beginning of a workday. The activity heightened my awareness that this was but a waystation in our travels. We quickened our pace, holding hands and laughing eagerly. We were headed for Marmaris. That was the important thing.

Henry has been making soups of late. He and Jeannie confer in the kitchen over our single burner as they take turns stirring the pot. Jeannie gets interrupted to make breakfast sandwiches for our customers, then comes back to the pot and peers in, muttering to herself about not remembering what she'd already put in. Henry goes off to slash the bread before putting it into the oven. He, too, tries to remember where they are with the soup. In this way a new recipe emerges. The kitchen fills with the aromas created by crushed herbs, sautéed vegetables, freshly chopped celery, diced hot peppers. Everything gets tossed in the pot. One morning as they are both peering at the simmering soup, he on one side of the burner, she on the other, I remember quite suddenly and vividly that morning 28 years ago when we were eating mercimek corbasi in a Turkish soup shop.

How far we've traveled. And yet here we still are. It is morning. We have soup, sustenance, and comfort. As we give you these soup recipes for the days ahead, we wish the same for you—perfect sustenance, complete comfort, and good cheer.

35

STARRY NIGHT CUCUMBER SOUP

Our favorite chilled soup is one Henry made many years ago for a special friend when we were living on the island of Nantucket.

Nantucketer Mark Duffield was a self-proclaimed connoisseur of chilled cucumber soup. An inveterate traveler, he had a wealth of stories to tell about hiking across Africa, boating up the Amazon, and refusing to be helicoptered off a sailboat during a tempest in the Bermuda Triangle. But though he had to be prodded to tell his adventurous tales, he could not be stopped from launching into panegyrics on the cucumber soup served at The Chanticleer, a French restaurant in the village of 'Sconset. Deciding to serve Mark a cucumber soup that would reduce him to silence on the subject of cucumber soup, we invited him and another friend to go picnicking with us on Madaket Beach.

It was a perfect Nantucket July night. The sun had set and the stars were popping out by the time we parked the car near the beach, which was flat and broad and easy to walk on. The air was cool and still. There was no moon, and no houses dimmed the starlight. We walked a while across the firm sand and then spread out our blankets, tablecloth, and picnic supplies. We had brought real silverware, glasses, china, and a set of candles. That morning we had baked baguettes of French bread. We lit the candles, set out the crusty loaves, a plate of unsalted butter, a bottle of chilled white wine, and a bouquet of bright Nantucket flowers. While I poured the wine, Henry ladled out the soup, which he had made early in the day from the cucumbers and asparagus tips purchased from the local farmer's stand on Broad Street.

The soup was creamy, cold, and utterly delicious. The fact that the night was cool enough for sweaters made us appreciate the soup even more than we might have in the middle of a hot sunny day. The cool taste on our tongues was in perfect harmony with the crisp air that brushed our hands and faces. We ate and drank in silent companionship under the immense canopy of the stars.

STARRY NIGHT CUCUMBER SOUP

1½ pounds cucumbers
½ pound tiny fresh
   asparagus
2 tablespoons butter
½ cup minced onions
4 tablespoons flour

6 cups light chicken broth
1½ teaspoons rice wine
   vinegar
1 cup half-and-half
1 cup sour cream
salt and pepper

Peel cucumbers. Cut 20 paper-thin slices and reserve. Cut the remaining cucumber into ½ inch chunks. Wash the asparagus, and holding with one hand on each end, bend the stalks until they break. Save the top halves (tender part) and discard the bottom parts. Cut the tender parts into one-inch segments, reserving the tips separately. In a skillet, cook the onions slowly in butter until tender. Add the flour and cook for one minute. Whisk in the chicken broth and bring to the boil over high heat. Add the cucumber chunks, asparagus segments and vinegar. Simmer, partially covered, for 15 minutes. Add the asparagus tips and cook 5 minutes more. With a slotted spoon remove the tips and reserve. Puree the soup in a food processor. Season with salt and pepper. Stir in the half-and-half and sour cream. Chill. Stir in the reserved asparagus tips. Serve in chilled bowls, floating the reserved cucumber slices on the top and placing a dollop of sour cream in the center.

WHITE BEAN, POTATO SOUP WITH PESTO

Henry created this soup with our Orange Blossom vegetarian friends in mind. The combination of hearty white beans and potatoes blended with the intense flavor of fresh basil produces a lusty soup that has no need of chicken or beef broth to produce a satisfying sense of repleteness.

The Soup

12 cups water
1 pound great northern
   beans
½ medium-size white onion,
   peeled

2 medium-size zucchini, diced
3 potatoes, peeled and diced
6 fresh plum tomatoes, diced
2½ teaspoons salt
¼ teaspoon black pepper

The Pesto

16 leaves of fresh basil
1 tablespoon garlic
½ teaspoon red pepper flakes

3 tablespoons extra-virgin
   olive oil

In a large pot, bring the water to the boil and stir in the beans. Return to the boil and simmer for one minute. Remove from the heat, cover, and let stand for one hour. Return to the heat, add the onion, and cook until the beans are almost tender. Discard the onion and add the potatoes, zucchini, tomatoes, salt and pepper. Simmer until the potatoes are tender. Puree the ingredients for the pesto in a food processor and stir into the simmering soup.

WHITE BEAN AND VEGETABLE SOUP WITH ARBORIO RICE AND PARMESAN CHEESE

½ pound white beans, soaked, drained, and rinsed
¼ cup olive oil
1 cup chopped onion
1 cup chopped celery
1 cup peeled and chopped carrots
1½ teaspoons minced garlic

2½ cups canned plum tomatoes, chopped, plus juice
4-6 cups water
½ cup Arborio rice
3 cups fresh spinach, washed, stemmed, and sliced
1 teaspoon salt
¼ teaspoon black pepper
grated Parmesan cheese

In a large heavy bottomed pot sauté the onion, celery, and carrot in olive oil for a few minutes. Stir in the garlic and cook for one minute. Add the white beans, tomatoes and 4 cups of water. Simmer, partially covered, until the beans are tender. Stir in the rice, salt, and pepper and cook for about 20 minutes (adding more water if necessary). Stir in the spinach and cook until it wilts. Serve with Parmesan cheese.

BEANS AND GREENS GUMBO

To qualify as a true Southerner, one must at some point come to terms with okra, that slimy-green seed-filled pod with the indescribable taste. As a child and young adult, I would only eat it fried. And it had to be dipped in cornmeal first, and so heavily salted and peppered that my mouth was on fire for thirty minutes afterward and my throat was parched with thirst even though I guzzled down at least three tall glasses of iced tea. I'm not certain when I accepted non-fried okra into my life. It probably happened around the same time that I gave up trying to rid myself of my twangy Western-North Carolina drawl. My one clear recollection is of seeking out a can of okra and tomatoes in the grocery store and suddenly realizing that my mouth was watering over the prospect of consuming stewed okra. Southern at last.

The standard Southern way of cooking okra is in a gumbo. Both the texture and the taste of okra stand up well to the spicy gumbo seasonings. Henry's gumbo takes advantage of the unique flavor and texture of another Southern staple, collard greens. I love the combination of collards and okra in this recipe, and I have never been able to stop with only a single bowlful of this nourishing, flavor-filled Southern standby.

BEANS AND GREENS GUMBO

½ pound great northern
    beans
6 cups water
¼ large white onion, peeled
10 large leaves of collard
    greens
2 tablespoons vegetable oil
2 stalks celery, diced
½ large green pepper, diced
1½ teaspoons minced garlic

½ cup frozen corn, defrosted
½ small package frozen cut
    okra, defrosted
1 10 ounce can diced
    tomatoes with green
    chilies
½ package Zatarain's New
    Orleans Style Gumbo Mix
    with Rice
½ teaspoon salt

Bring the water to the boil and add the beans. Return to the boil and cook for one minute. Remove from the heat, cover, and let stand for one hour. Add the onion and return to the boil. Reduce heat and simmer until the beans are half cooked. Cut the collard green leaves off the tough center stems and add to the beans. Simmer until the beans are tender. Discard the onion. Sauté the celery, green pepper, and garlic in vegetable oil for a few minutes and add to the beans along with the corn, okra, and the tomatoes with green chilies. Stir in the gumbo seasoning mix and salt and cook for about 20 minutes. Serve with a scoop of rice.

PEAS PORRIDGE HOT

There's no better soup to serve on a frigid February day - but it's also fresh and refreshing enough to serve on a midsummer's night.

1½ cups diced onion
1 cup diced celery
2 tablespoons olive oil
1 teaspoon minced garlic
¾ cup split peas
2 cups chicken stock
4 cups water
2 cups peeled and diced
    potatoes
2 cups diced zucchini

12 ounces fresh spinach,
    washed well, stems
    removed
⅛ teaspoon thyme
⅛ teaspoon cayenne pepper
2 teaspoons salt (use less if
    stock is salted)
¼ cup chopped fresh parsley
lemon wedges
sour cream

Sauté the onion and celery in olive oil. Add the garlic, split peas, stock, 2 cups of water and potatoes. Simmer, covered, for 40 minutes. Add the zucchini, spinach, seasonings, and remaining 2 cups of water. Cook for about 10 minutes, until the zucchini is tender. Puree the soup in a food processor. Upon serving the soup, garnish each bowl with chopped parsley and a dollop of sour cream. Serve with lemon wedges.

BLACK BEAN CHILE

The texture, taste, and character of this chile are entirely dependent on the use of Henry's Black Bean recipe (See our Mexican specialties section), so please don't be tempted to substitute canned black beans or a bland home-cooked version. When serving this popular dish at The Orange Blossom, we add a scoopful of plain boiled rice. By adding a slightly sweet corn muffin on the side, one achieves a perfect balancing of protein and a perfectly satisfying combination of flavors.

¼ cup olive oil
3 cups chopped white onion
2 cups chopped red bell
    pepper
2 large jalapeños, finely
    chopped
1 tablespoon minced garlic
1 tablespoon paprika
2 teaspoons cumin

2 teaspoons pure red chile
    powder
1 teaspoon oregano
3 cups canned tomatoes,
    chopped, with juice
10 cups freshly cooked black
    beans (see recipe page
    108)
1 teaspoon red wine vinegar

Sauté the onion, bell pepper, jalapeño, garlic, and seasonings in olive oil for a few minutes. Add the tomatoes, black beans, and vinegar and simmer for 15 minutes. Serve with chopped red onion, salsa, sour cream, and grated cheddar cheese.

VEGETARIAN CHILE

A friend of ours, Honest Bill Crook, grows habañero peppers, also known as Scotch Bonnets, in his island garden. He does not eat them, nor the serrano peppers and jalapeños he also grows.

Pepper plants are beautiful to look at, especially the habañeros with their orange, benignly beautiful fruit. When Bill first presented us with a zip-lock freezer bag filled with the orange habañeros, we were tempted to do no more than look. Though we have long made liberal use of serranos and jalapeños in our cooking and sparing use of habañero sauce, we had never even thought of adding a fresh habañero to anything. After all, who wants or needs one-thousand times more heat than a jalapeño offers? But we didn't like the thought of Bill's lovely orange fruit going to waste, so we decided to add a bit (?) of extra zip to Henry's vegetarian chile, in which he normally used jalapeños or serranos. We discovered that by cooking the habañero in the chile and then discarding the cooked pepper before serving, the tantalizing flavor of the habañero comes through, and a wonderful warmth pervades each taste, without one having to suffer the shocking burn from biting into a chunk of Scotch Bonnet.

Around the time we were experimenting with habañeros, the Cape Hatteras School was sponsoring a chile-cook-off competition for island restaurants. We entered this chile, never thinking it would win over the traditional meat chile, but it did, which may be partially because of the unique flavor added by the habañero. Also important to the substantial taste of the dish is the black-eyed peas as a meat substitute.

VEGETARIAN CHILE

½ pound dried red kidney beans
½ pound dried black-eyed peas
½ cup diced white onion
1 tablespoon red chile powder
1 teaspoon dry mustard
1 teaspoon salt
¾ teaspoon cumin
¾ teaspoon oregano
¾ teaspoon cayenne pepper
½ teaspoon paprika
½ teaspoon black pepper
½ teaspoon onion powder
½ teaspoon garlic powder
¼ teaspoon white pepper
¼ cup rice wine
2 tablespoons soy sauce
1 can Rotel tomatoes with green chilies
1 can stewed tomatoes with Mexican seasonings
2 stalks celery, diced
1 habañero pepper

In a large heavy bottomed pot bring 10 cups of water to the boil. Add the beans, bring back to the boil, and simmer for a few minutes. Remove from the heat, cover, and let stand for 2 hours. Add all of the remaining ingredients except the celery and habañero pepper. Bring to the boil, reduce heat, and simmer, partially covered, for 1 hour. Add the celery and habañero pepper and simmer, partially covered, until the beans are tender, adding more water if necessary. Discard the habañero pepper. Serve with a scoop of plain boiled rice, salsa, sour cream, and grated sharp cheddar cheese.

AUTUMN VEGETABLE CHOWDER

Autumn Vegetable Chowder is the most requested soup at the Orange Blossom. We serve it year-round, simply changing the name of the vegetables to suit the season.

A note of caution in serving the soup; it tends to curdle if it is kept over too high heat for very long, so it is best to serve it as soon as possible after heating.

6 tablespoons butter
1½ cups diced white onion
½ cup minced scallion
1 cup diced sweet red
   pepper
1 zucchini, diced
2 carrots, peeled and diced
4 baking potatoes, peeled
   and diced
1 tablespoon salt
½ teaspoon black pepper

2 cups water
5 cups milk
2 cups half-and-half
2 tablespoons flour
3 cups frozen corn
1 cup frozen sliced okra
1 cup frozen sugar snaps
2 cups grated Mexican
   Velveeta cheese
paprika

In a large heavy bottomed pot, combine the butter, onion, scallions, red pepper, zucchini, carrots, potatoes, water, salt and pepper. Bring to the boil, reduce heat, and simmer, partially covered, until the potatoes are barely tender. In a separate saucepan, combine the half-and-half with four cups of milk and heat until almost boiling. Whisk together the flour and remaining cup of milk and whisk into the hot liquid. Whisk the mixture to the boil and add the corn, okra, and sugar snaps. Return to the boil and add to the potato mixture. Stir everything together over moderate heat and bring almost to the boil. Remove from the heat and stir in the cheese. Sprinkle with paprika and serve.

CORN CHOWDER

¾ stick butter
1½ cups diced onion
½ cup finely chopped green onion
1 cup diced sweet red pepper
2 serrano chilies, minced (optional)

4 cups peeled and cubed potatoes
5 cups corn kernels (freshly cut off the cob)
4 tablespoons flour
6 cups whole milk
⅛ teaspoon cayenne pepper
⅛ teaspoon black pepper
2 teaspoons salt

Melt the butter in a large heavy-bottomed pot and cook the onions, scallions, red pepper, and chilies until barely tender. Whisk in the flour and stir over moderate heat for one minute. Whisk in the cold milk and continue whisking over high heat to the boil. Stir in the potatoes and seasonings. Lower the heat and simmer, partially covered, until the potatoes are almost tender. Add the corn and continue cooking until the potatoes are completely tender. Remove from the heat. Serve with hot cornbread and a garden salad.

GAZPACHO

2 tablespoons olive oil
2 tablespoons vegetable oil
1 cup diced white onion
3 small scallions, minced
1 clove of garlic, minced
4 cups diced fresh tomatoes
2½ green peppers, diced
2½ tender stalks celery, diced
3 peeled, seeded and chopped cucumbers

1 small carrot, peeled and diced
½ bunch of parsley, chopped
2 cups tomato juice
1 tablespoon vinaigrette
1 teaspoon dried basil
1½ teaspoons sugar
1½ teaspoons salt
½ teaspoon pepper
⅛ teaspoon hot sauce
1 cup mild chicken stock

Cook the onions, scallions, and garlic briefly in oil. Cool completely. In a large bowl mix together the remaining ingredients and stir into the onion mixture. Refrigerate for at least 4 hours.

PEARL OF A SOUP

Clams, red chilies, and red wine make for a perfect combination of heat and rich flavor in this wonderful soup, which is quite simply one of the best dishes I've ever tasted. Toss a salad, open a bottle of robust wine, and tear off hunks of crusty French bread to sop up every last taste of broth.

2 tablespoons olive oil
1 medium white onion,
    finely chopped
1 tablespoon minced garlic
4 cups canned tomatoes,
    diced, with juice
¾ cup dry red wine
¼ cup chopped parsley

2 teaspoons dried basil
½ teaspoon black pepper
2 dozen small clams, washed
    well
salt to taste
red chile pesto (see
    following recipe)

In a large non-aluminum saucepan, sauté the onion in olive oil until soft. Add the garlic and cook, stirring, for one minute. Add the tomatoes with their juice, red wine, herbs, chile seeds, and pepper. Bring to a boil, lower the heat and simmer gently, partially covered, for a few hours. Before serving return to the boil and stir in the red chile pesto. Add the clams, cover, and cook until the clams open.

Red Chile Pesto

1 2-ounce package of New
    Mexico dried red chiles
¼ cup olive oil

1 tablespoon minced garlic
½ cup grated Parmesan
    cheese

Remove the stems from the chilies and shake out the seeds into a fine sieve. Rinse the seeds under cold water and reserve. Wash the chilies under cold water, tear into pieces, and place in a small bowl. Pour over 2 cups boiling water, cover, and let the chilies soak for 15 minutes or longer. Drain, reserving the liquid. Place the chilies in a blender, add 1 cup of the reserved liquid, and blend to a smooth consistency. Strain the puree into a bowl using a fine sieve and pressing on the chilies with the back of a rubber spatula. Discard the skins which remain in the sieve. Place the chile puree back into the blender, add the remaining ingredients along with the reserved seeds and blend.

FRESH AND CREAMY CLAM CHOWDER

The name chowder is derived from the French *chaudière*, a cauldron that was used in French fishing villages for communal fish soups. Individual fishermen put part of their catch into the *chaudière* to make a rich community stew from all the fish and shellfish available in the sea.

The most common chowder in this country is based on clams, salt pork, onions, and potatoes; and of this type there are three basic versions: the New England or Nantucket, the Manhattan, and the Hatteras. The first is made with milk, the second with tomatoes, and the third with neither, which is the Hatterasman's individualistic way of dispensing with the great chowder controversy that has raged for generations between New Yorkers and New Englanders regarding the merits of milk and tomatoes in relationship to clams. In omitting both the milk and the tomatoes, the Hatteras Islander's chowder more closely resembles the original version which was simmered in the *chaudières* of Breton fishing villages. We prefer the Nantucket style chowder, but one can make a fine Hatteras chowder by omitting the flour and cream from the following recipe, and whisking four tablespoons of cornmeal into the simmering soup and cooking five minutes extra to allow the broth to thicken slightly.

When we were working at the Club Car Restaurant in Nantucket, the chef, Frank Young, used to make an excellent Nantucket chowder using a different method from the one described below. He never chopped his clams. Instead, he bought fresh shucked clams which he put through a food grinder. He did the same with the potatoes, scrubbing them diligently and leaving the peel on. The peels added a stronger potato flavor. The chowder, which he prepared with milk rather than cream, was delicious, but the ground-up potato skins gave it a slightly grayish cast that was not appealing.

Frank was the person who taught Henry how to handle Nantucket chowder after it is cooked. A young, enthusiastic, and boundlessly energetic cook in those days, Henry could not have been expected to comprehend the weary wisdom of an old chef. In hindsight, I think it safe to say that just the sight of Henry's alert and eager face on an early Sunday morning after one of those endless summer-Saturday nights spent serving up sautéed seafood and Caesar salad to well-heeled tourists—just the sight of that cheerful, ready-to-tackle-the-world countenance must have inclined an already overworked and sleep-deprived Frank to retire to his bed for the remainder of the day.

At the end of one particularly exhausting Saturday night when Frank slumped out the kitchen door, barely able to hold his throbbing head up and his beer belly in, Henry, who was still bustling about the kitchen, decided to help Frank out by making the chowder for him. What a happy surprise Frank would have when he entered the kitchen early Sunday morning, which was Frank's chowder-making day, to discover that the tedious task had already been accomplished for him. Henry knew the method. He knew the proportions. He stayed late into the night laboring over an enormous stockpot filled with Frank's wonderful chowder. When at long last the chowder was done, Henry manhandled the stockpot into the walk-in refrigerator, covered the pot securely, and congratulated himself on his efforts as he imagined Frank's expression upon entering the walk-in a few hours hence.

It was so late by the time Henry got to bed that he was not on hand to see Frank's expression on Sunday morning. Which was probably just as well. For what Henry did not then know was the cardinal rule for handling chowder: Never cover the pot while the chowder cools. It will go sour. And it did. All that lovely, huge stockpot filled with Henry's energetic efforts. Frank tossed it out Sunday morning.

But on Monday he didn't say a word. Henry couldn't understand Frank's silence, his strange lack of gratitude, so finally he asked.

"I threw it out," was Frank's reply.

Henry gaped, then repeated, "Threw it out?!"

"It went bad."

Still Frank refrained from elaborating. One can imagine that he had done all of his elaborating early Sunday morning, alone there in the walk-in, with only a pot-full of sour chowder to hear him.

Finally, Henry, still not really believing, managed to extract from Frank the facts of chowder life: One must cool chowder completely before refrigerating.

When cooling, place the pot on a wire rack so that the air can circulate underneath. If a skin forms on top, skim it off. And cover *only after* the chowder is thoroughly cooled.

One further note on making cream-based clam chowder. Sometimes here at the Orange Blossom we add a touch of chicken base. This makes for a richer soup which the customers love.

FRESH AND CREAMY CLAM CHOWDER

2 strips salt pork, cut into
    small pieces, or 3
    tablespoons butter
½ cup finely chopped onion
4 tablespoons flour
4 cups peeled and diced
    potatoes

12 large cherrystone clams,
    or enough to yield 3 cups
    of chopped clams with
    juice
3½ cups water
2 cups half-and-half
½ teaspoon black pepper
paprika

Wash the clams under cold running water while scrubbing vigorously with a stiff brush to remove sand and grit. Freeze the washed clams. After the clams are thoroughly frozen, remove them from the freezer and cover with hot water. This immersion causes the clams to open just enough for you to cut easily around the shells with a knife, severing the muscles that hold them closed. Cut out the clams with their frozen juices and place in a bowl. Cut away any greenish areas on the clams. Chop the frozen clams on a board, being careful to save the icy clam juice. Set aside 3 cups of clams plus juice. Freeze the excess. If using salt pork, cook over medium heat in a heavy-bottomed pot until the fat is rendered and the pork is lightly browned. Discard the pork, add the onions to the pan, and cook until soft (if using butter, melt in pan and cook onions until soft over medium heat.) Whisk in the flour and cook for one minute. Add the 3 cups of reserved clams, clam juice, water, and potatoes and stir to the boil. Reduce heat and simmer, partially covered, until the potatoes are tender. In a separate pan, warm the half-and-half and add to the chowder. Remove from the heat and season with black pepper. Sprinkle with paprika.

SHRIMP, CORN AND CLAM CHOWDER

3 tablespoons butter
¾ cup chopped onion
¼ cup finely chopped
   scallions
¾ cup chopped sweet red
   pepper
¼ cup flour
1¾ cups clam juice
3 potatoes, peeled and diced

2 cups corn
2½ cups milk
1 cup half-and-half
1 cup canned clams
½ pound peeled and
   deveined shrimp
½ teaspoon black pepper
½ teaspoon salt

Sauté the vegetables in butter. Stir in the flour and cook for one minute. Add the clam juice and whisk to the boil. Add the potatoes, partially cover, and simmer until the potatoes are tender. Add the milk, half-and-half, and corn and bring almost to the boil. Add the shrimp, clams, black pepper and salt. Cook, stirring, over low heat, until the seafood is cooked through but still tender. Remove from the heat and serve with a sprinkling of paprika.

ORANGE BLOSSOM KITCHEN CHOWDER

Seafood Stock

4 cups clam juice
4 cups water
4 cloves garlic, peeled and
  crushed
½ teaspoon oregano

1 bay leaf
1 pound snow crab legs
½ pound shrimp in the shell,
  rinsed

Combine water, clam juice, garlic and seasonings in a large pot. Bring to a boil and add the crab legs. Reduce the heat to simmer and cook 12 minutes. Remove crab and reserve. Add shrimp to the pot and cook until they are pink and curled. Remove shrimp and reserve. Strain and reserve stock. Remove the crab from the shell, peel the shrimp, and set aside.

The Chowder

¼ cup olive oil
8 whole cloves garlic, peeled
½ teaspoon cayenne pepper
1 cup sliced onion
½ large red bell pepper,
  chopped
½ large green bell pepper,
  chopped
1 cup canned plum tomatoes,
  chopped, with juice

3 cups peeled and diced
  potatoes
½ teaspoon oregano
½ pound boneless, skinless
  fish filets, cut into bite-
  size pieces
reserved shrimp and
  crabmeat
reserved stock

In a large heavy-bottomed pot, lightly sauté the garlic and cayenne pepper in olive oil, being careful not to brown. Add onion, red and green pepper, cover, and cook on low until soft. Add tomatoes, potatoes and reserved stock. Cook until the potatoes are tender. Add the fish and cook until white and flaky. Add the reserved shrimp and crabmeat and cook 1 minute more. Serve with French bread and a garden salad.

SEAFOOD CHOWDER

4 tablespoons butter
1 cup chopped onion
1 cup chopped celery
¼ cup chopped sweet red
    pepper
½ cup flour
4½ cups clam juice
3 baking potatoes, peeled
    and diced
½ pound peeled and
    deveined shrimp

½ pound scallops
½ pound Rock Fish, skinned,
    boned, and cut into bite-
    size pieces (other white
    meat fish may be
    substituted)
1 cup half-and-half
½ teaspoon black pepper
paprika

Sauté the onions, celery, and red pepper in butter until the onions are translucent. Whisk in the flour and cook, stirring, for one minute. Whisk in the clam juice and bring to the boil. Add the potatoes and simmer, partially covered, until the potatoes are barely tender. Add the seafood and simmer for a few minutes until cooked through but still tender. Remove from the heat. In a separate pan warm the half-and-half and stir into the chowder. Sprinkle with paprika.

SOUTHERN SMOOTH SHE-CRAB SOUP

5 tablespoons butter
1 medium onion, peeled and
    sliced
4 cups half-and-half
1 bay leaf
4 tablespoons flour
1 teaspoon salt
⅛ teaspoon cayenne pepper

½ teaspoon nutmeg
½ teaspoon Worcestershire
    sauce
¾ pound lump crab meat,
    picked through to
    remove all shell
4 tablespoons dry sherry
paprika

In a heavy-bottomed pot, cook the onion in 1 tablespoon of butter until soft. Add the cream and bay leaf, bring to a boil, reduce the heat, and simmer for 10 minutes. Strain and reserve the liquid. Melt the remaining 4 tablespoons of butter in the pot, whisk in the flour and cook for 1 minute. Whisk in the reserved liquid and seasonings, bring to a boil, reduce the heat to simmer, and add the crab. Cook on very low heat to heat the crab through. Place 1 tablespoon of sherry in each soup bowl. Ladle in the soup and dust with paprika.

Salads and Sides

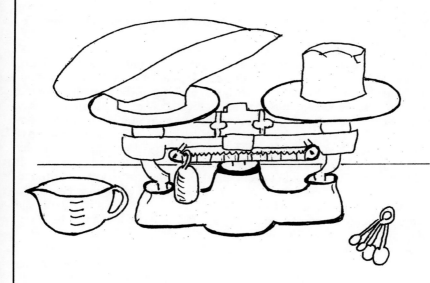

The old baker's scale
still works.

ADVENTURES IN MEASURES

Every once in a while I come across one of those recipe-metaphor po-ems, in a churchwomen's spiral-bound volume of favorite recipes, or in a women's magazine. They usually have titles like "recipe for living," "recipe for a happy home," "recipe for love." There is a basic wholesomeness in their ingredients, and an uncomplicated wisdom in their directions. Though I never seem to have the requisite ingredients on hand, I can always relate to the way the measurements are given out in the typically imprecise language of the home-cook: a dollop of this, a dash of that, a pinch of one thing, a handful of another.

I am not certain whether it is a masculine trait to rely on accurate measures—like teaspoons, cups, and quarts—and a feminine trait to pre-fer dollops, dashes, and handfuls; or whether it simply happens that the individual male cooks I've known and worked with are measurers while the females are not. Be that as it may, somewhere along the line I've acquired the notion that men are, by nature, measurers and women, by nature, are not.

My idea holds true in The Orange Blossom kitchen, where Henry in-vests a considerable amount of energy into checking to see that Ruth, Jeannie, and I are measuring accurately. It is a constant battle. In some skirmishes he admits defeat, as with the making of the icing for glazing the turnovers, Danishes, and sweet rolls. Ruth makes the icing perfectly every day. For a long while, Henry insisted that she measure out the proportion of water to confectioner's sugar, his reasoning being that any-one else would then be able to make up the icing. This, after all, is why recipes are written—so that other people can do them. But whenever Ruth tried to measure, she couldn't seem to get the icing the way she wanted it. And it took three times as long. Eventually the two of them arrived at a truce, whereby Ruth agreed to use the mixer instead of stirring up the sugar and water by hand, and Henry agreed never to bring up the ques-tion of measuring the icing again.

Jeannie, one of the most talented cooks I've ever known, understands the logic behind measuring. She understands, for example, the impor-tance of accurate measurements in areas such as bread and cake baking, where too much or too little yeast or baking powder or salt can ruin the end product. She knows it, but she freely admits that in her own home kitchen, she never measures anything. Every morning when she comes to work, she gathers measuring devices on her worktable—spoons, third-cups, half-cups, pints, quarts. She jokes about her array, saying that she's hoarding her supplies. With dogged determination, she moves through the morning, measuring. The fact that measuring is an unnatural activ-ity for her becomes apparent in the very care she takes to be perfectly accurate.

Whenever I see her studying the water line in a clear-plastic quart measure as she attempts to judge whether or not she has exactly 3 cups of liquid, I feel a sudden pang of empathy at the expression of mistrust on her face; for I, too, have a tendency to doubt the evidence before my eyes when it comes to measures. Three cupfuls in a narrow measure is not always quite the same as it is in a wide one, and then, too, when measuring liquids there is the consideration of whether the measuring device is sitting on a level surface. Professional bakers most often weigh their liquid ingredients instead of measuring them. My friend and mentor, Allan Oakham, was fond of saying to me, "A pint's a pound the world around." But I have never really been convinced of this truth, any more than I have succeeded in convincing myself that measures really work.

Like Jeannie, whenever I am left to my own devices, I tend to dispense with measurements, which in my case sometimes results in the inability to duplicate a recipe that turned out well the first time, though it undoubtedly allows for a kind of spontaneous flow in the original act of creation. Sometimes I find myself wishing that I could attend to my measuring better, as in the example of the Fabulous Fiber Salad.

I first made it last winter when I happened to notice a package of 15-variety dried beans and a box of bulgur wheat-and-orzo pilaf nestled side-by-side in my shopping cart, and the thought occurred to me that they might go well together in a tabouli-like salad, but without the cloying taste of the mint usually found in tabouli. When I got home, I cooked the beans and pilaf separately, then drained the beans and tossed them into the pilaf along with parsley, tomatoes, cucumbers, red pepper, lemon juice, salt, and plenty of black pepper. The results were tasty, nutritious, and satisfying.

When we opened the bakery for the season, I decided to make the salad for a lunch special. Having only a single box of pilaf on hand, I knew I would have to stretch the ingredients some way or other, so I cooked additional orzo pasta and some brown rice and tossed them in with the original ingredients, along with some added salt and pepper. Upon Henry's suggestion I also added some of our balsamic vinaigrette. The entire time I worked, I had one eye on the clock, for the salad had to be finished by lunchtime, and I paid not a whit of attention to how much of what was going into the salad. The results were even nicer than the first time. Later, when a customer requested that I make the Fabulous Fiber Salad again, the only thing that came to mind was the memory of flying around the kitchen to obtain a handful of this, a dollop of that, and a pinch and a dash of something else. The litany that Henry recites daily began to ring in my ears: "Take time to measure!" and "Write down what you do!"

Well, I went back, I measured, I wrote it all down. I still like the recipe, and I think perhaps that anyone else tasting the results would not be able to tell the difference between this newer version and the original one. After mulling it over, I've come to the conclusion that the reason I liked the first one better was because the process itself was such an adventure—and adventure is not something one can measure.

FABULOUS FIBER SALAD

Although when I originally made the salad, I used a box of Near East Bulgur Wheat Pilaf Mix, when I wanted to do the salad a second time, I could not find this mix in any of the stores on the Outer Banks. If the mix is available where you live, cook according to package directions and add to the remaining ingredients in the recipe. If it is unavailable, cook 1 cup of raw bulgur wheat with ½ cup chopped onions, 1 teaspoon minced garlic, 1 teaspoon salt, and 2 cups of boiling water for 20 minutes. Drain and cool to room temperature, then add to the remaining salad ingredients.

1 box of Near East Bulgur Wheat Pilaf Mix, cooked according to package instructions
15-variety dried beans, rinsed, soaked, cooked until tender, and drained, enough to make 3 cups of cooked beans
2 cups cooked orzo pasta
2 cups cooked brown rice
3 cups diced fresh tomatoes
2 cups peeled and diced cucumbers

½ cup diced sweet red pepper
½ cup minced green onion, green portion included
¼ cup minced fresh parsley
4 teaspoons salt
½ teaspoon black pepper
2 tablespoons fresh lemon juice
¼ cup balsamic vinaigrette (see recipe page 86) or vinaigrette of choice

Toss the above ingredients and chill before serving.

58

JANUARY FRIED RICE SALAD

January is the month when fresh locally grown collards are available on our grocery shelves here on Hatteras Island. They are delicious in fried rice. The following recipe is hot, but it is a flavor-filled heat supplied by the habañero pepper and it is guaranteed to have people asking for second and third helpings. Though we like heat in our food, we used to be wary of using the habañero (or Scotch Bonnet, as it is also called). A gardener friend of ours began to supply us with the beautiful orange habañeros from his garden, and we discovered that we could use them without burning people out as long as we were careful to remove all the seeds and veins before mincing.

2 tablespoons olive oil
1 teaspoon minced garlic
1½ teaspoons minced fresh
   ginger
½ cup chopped scallions
   (including the green tops)
½ teaspoon minced fresh
   habañero pepper, or 1
   teaspoon minced fresh
   jalapeño, if habañero is
   unavailable
1 cup diced sweet red pepper
½ cup carrots, sliced on the
   diagonal

½ cup thinly sliced celery
½ cup sugar snaps
1 cup cooked black beans (see
   recipe page 108), drained
   and lightly rinsed
½ cup frozen corn kernels
1 cup sliced cooked fresh
   collards
1 tablespoon lime juice
2 tablespoons soy sauce
1 tablespoon black bean
   sauce (if available)
3 cups cooked white rice

Heat olive oil in wok or a large nonstick skillet. Stir-fry garlic, ginger, scallions, and habañero pepper for 15 seconds. Add red pepper, carrot, celery, and sugar snaps. Stir-fry for 2 to 3 minutes. Meanwhile toss together in a bowl the black beans, corn kernels, collards, and lime juice. Add to the frying vegetables and stir in the soy sauce and black bean sauce. Stir-fry for 2 minutes, then add the rice and toss while continuing to cook until the rice is heated.

ORIENTAL BROWN RICE SALAD

4 cups cooked brown rice
1 cup peeled and diced
  cucumber
1 cup diced sweet red
  pepper
1 cup cooked kernel corn,
  cooled
1 cup sugar snap peas,
  cooked and cooled
1 cup diced red onion
1 serrano chile, finely
  minced
3 tablespoons olive oil

2 tablespoons rice wine
  vinegar
2 tablespoons lemon juice
1 tablespoon hot soy sauce
1 tablespoon sugar
1 tablespoon chopped
  parsley
1½ teaspoons salt
⅛ teaspoon black pepper
⅛ teaspoon cayenne pepper
¼ cup balsamic vinaigrette
  (see recipe page 86)

Combine the rice and vegetables in a large mixing bowl. Whisk together the olive oil, rice wine vinegar, lemon juice, soy sauce, sugar, parsley, salt, black pepper, and cayenne pepper. Pour over the rice and vegetables and mix well. Stir in balsamic vinaigrette to taste and serve chilled.

BLACK BEAN AND YELLOW CORN SALAD

2 cups cooked and drained
  black beans (see recipe
  page 108)
1 cup frozen yellow corn
  kernels, defrosted and
  drained
½ cup finely chopped red
  onion

1 cup cubed roma tomatoes
3 tablespoons vegetable oil
2 tablespoons rice wine
  vinegar
2 tablespoons fresh lime juice
1 teaspoon salt
⅛ teaspoon black pepper
⅛ teaspoon cayenne pepper

Combine ingredients in a large bowl and refrigerate. Bring back to room temperature before serving.

FOURTH OF JULY POTATO SALAD

4 cups peeled and cubed potatoes, cooked tender in boiling salted water, drained and rinsed
½ cup finely chopped green pepper
½ cup finely chopped sweet red pepper
⅓ cup finely chopped red onion
1 hard boiled egg, minced
1 tablespoon Dijonnaise mustard
½ cup mayonnaise
2 teaspoons rice wine vinegar
1 teaspoon salt
½ teaspoon black pepper

Combine ingredients in a large bowl and mix together well. Refrigerate for several hours before serving.

MEDITERRANEAN POTATO AND PASTA SALAD

4 cups peeled and cubed potatoes, cooked tender in boiling salted water, drained
1 can garbanzo beans, drained and rinsed
1 package frozen green beans, defrosted in hot water and drained
2 cups finely chopped celery
1 cup grated carrot
½ large sweet red pepper, finely chopped
1 cup diced roma tomatoes
1½ cups finely chopped red onion
1 small package shell pasta, cooked tender in boiling salted water, drained and rinsed
2 cloves garlic, peeled and minced in ½ teaspoon salt
2 teaspoons dried basil
2 teaspoons red wine vinegar
1 tablespoon salt
1½ teaspoons black pepper
½ teaspoon red pepper flakes
1 cup (or more) mayonnaise

Combine ingredients in a bowl and mix together well. Refrigerate for at least 4 hours before serving.

SUMMER FIESTA SALAD

1 cup canned garbanzo beans, drained and rinsed
1 cup canned red kidney beans, drained and rinsed
1 cup frozen corn, defrosted
1 cup frozen sugar snaps, defrosted
½ red onion, cut into thin rings
½ sweet red bell pepper, cut into rings

2 cups rotelle pasta, cooked, drained and rinsed
¼ cup rice wine vinegar
2 tablespoons vegetable oil
2 tablespoons sugar
1 teaspoon Dijon mustard
½ teaspoon dried basil
¼ teaspoon dried oregano
1 teaspoon salt
½ teaspoon coarse ground black pepper
½ cup balsamic vinaigrette (see recipe page 86)

Combine the vegetables and pasta in a large bowl. Whisk together the rice wine vinegar, oil, sugar, mustard, basil, oregano, salt, black pepper, and vinaigrette. Pour the dressing over the salad and mix well.

MACARONI SALAD

4 cups small shell pasta, cooked tender in boiling salted water, drained and rinsed
¾ cup finely chopped celery
⅔ cup grated carrot
3 tablespoons finely minced white onion
½ cup mayonnaise

2 hard boiled eggs, minced
2 teaspoons Dijonnaise mustard
½ teaspoon sugar
½ teaspoon salt
⅛ teaspoon black pepper
a few shakes of cayenne pepper
a few shakes of garlic salt

Combine ingredients in a bowl and mix together well. Refrigerate before serving.

SHRIMP AND PASTA SALAD

4 cups cooked pasta twists
2 cups small shrimp, cooked,
    peeled and deveined
¾ cup finely chopped celery
6 tablespoons finely
    chopped red onion
½ cup mayonnaise
2 teaspoons Dijonnaise
    mustard

¼ teaspoon garlic salt
¼ teaspoon salt
⅛ teaspoon each cayenne
    and black pepper
¼ teaspoon hot sauce
1 hard boiled egg, finely
    chopped

Mix ingredients together in a large bowl. Chill before serving.

FRESH TUNA SALAD

1 pound very fresh,
    boneless, skinless, tuna
4 cups water
1 tablespoon salt
½ cup chopped white onion
½ cup finely chopped kosher
    dill pickle

¼ cup finely chopped sweet
    red pepper
¾ cup mayonnaise
½ teaspoon salt
¼ teaspoon cayenne pepper

Rinse the tuna under cold running water. In a large pot, bring 4 cups of water to the boil. Add 1 tablespoon of salt and the tuna. Simmer until the tuna is tender (approximately 15 minutes). Drain, cool, and shred the tuna. Place in a mixing bowl. Pour 1 cup of boiling water over the onion and let stand for 10 minutes. Drain and rinse the onion under cold water. Combine the onion and remaining ingredients with the tuna. Chill before serving.

SWEET AND SOUR SLAW

1 pound packaged shredded
   cabbage mix
¼ cup finely chopped sweet
   red pepper
¼ cup finely chopped red
   onion
¼ cup finely chopped celery
   heart

1 large clove of garlic,
   minced in 1 teaspoon salt
2 tablespoons sugar
2 tablespoons cider vinegar
2 tablespoons vegetable oil
½ teaspoon black pepper

In a large bowl mix together the cabbage, vegetables, garlic and salt. Whisk together the sugar, vinegar, oil, and black pepper and pour over the cabbage and vegetables. Refrigerate until serving time.

FRISCO BEACH HASTY BAKED BEANS

1 30-ounce can pork and
   beans
1 cup finely chopped onion,
   sautéed in 1 tablespoon
   vegetable oil
½ cup ketchup
1 tablespoon mustard

¼ cup molasses
3 tablespoons brown sugar
2 teaspoons cider vinegar
¼ teaspoon salt
6 strips bacon, cooked crisp
½ teaspoon black pepper

Combine all ingredients, except bacon, and pour into a microwaveable casserole dish. Layer the top with strips of bacon. Cook for 15 minutes at 80% power, turning the casserole once. Lower to 60% power and cook for 10 more minutes. When using a conventional oven, bake for 1 hour at 350 degrees.

Sandwiches

The ticket spindle is full!

SAME DOUGH

During a December stay with Henry's brother and sister-in-law, Jim and Barbara Schliff of Scotia, New York, we made a mission of visiting bread bakeries in the Schenectady-Albany area. Most of the old-time ethnic Italian bake shops in Schenectady, where Henry grew up, have long since given way to the shiny automated bakeries housed in the Walmart-sized supermarkets located in affluent suburban communities like Scotia.

Price Chopper was the mega-market where Jim and Barbara did their shopping. It sprawled over acres of ground and was open twenty-four hours a day.

The mega-market was not on our list of neighborhood bakeries to visit, but one day when we were cooking Italian peppers, we decided we couldn't eat them without a loaf of Italian bread. Price Chopper was only minutes away.

Upon entering Price Chopper's bakery department, I quickly found myself losing all sense of original purpose as I stared at row upon row of artfully arranged display cases, bins, racks, islands and shelves, all loaded with apparently every type of bread that bakers had ever devised. The bakery itself was housed behind a wall of plate-glass windows. One could watch workers going about their activities in an immaculate, apparently flour-free environment. Stainless steel surfaces gleamed with a mirror shine.

As I began to drift aimlessly from case to case, I recognized but was powerless to prevent each succeeding symptom of the "This is Too Much!" syndrome which had begun to set in. My limbs grew heavy; my eyes glazed over; my mind shut down. Henry, at my side, was suffering from the same affliction, but he, unlike me, retained enough presence of mind to remember our original purpose.

"Let's find the Italian bread and get out of here," he said.

We began to look for Italian bread. Incredibly, we found none. After several minutes of fruitless searching, I was more than willing to give up, but Henry persisted, seeking out assistance from a clerk who directed us to a narrow bin where a single loaf of Italian bread lay sandwiched between other more exotic, ingeniously braided loaves.

The Italian bread was even-grained, smooth-skinned, obviously fresh. There was nothing to object to in it and nothing to remember about it.

After our lunch of peppers-and-provolone sandwiches, Jim mentioned that we should really try a loaf of Italian bread from Pirecca's Bakery in the old downtown section of Schenectady. Pirecca's was a Schenectady institution which had been in operation since the 1920's and remained a thriving business even as the old neighborhood and an entire way of life collapsed around it. The bakery had recently received an added boost to its prestige when Jack Nicholson, while on location for shooting a film, had grown so attached to Pirecca's bread that he made arrangements for a weekly supply of it to be flown in to his Hollywood home.

Jim knew that Pirecca's usually sold out its bread fairly early in the day, but he wasn't certain what time the shop opened. In vain we searched the pages of the telephone directory, looking under every imaginable spelling of Pirecca's. Finally Henry and Jim decided to drive into Schenectady to see if the hours were posted on the door. They were not. So the next morning the two of them went out at 7:30 and arrived just as a batch of Italian bread was coming out of the oven.

A lone clerk was in the front of the small shop. Fascinated by a sheet pan filled with aromatic, just-baked "pizza bread," Henry inquired of the clerk if the dough for the pizza bread were different from the refrigerated bags of fresh pizza dough that were for sale.

The clerk looked at him. "Same dough," she acknowledged.

Henry bought a package of the fresh dough, several squares of the puffy pizza bread, one baguette and two rounds of the freshly-baked, still hot Italian loaves. "How about the Italian rounds?" he asked the clerk. "Is that a different dough from the pizza?"

"Same dough," the clerk said.

"And the baguettes?" Henry persisted, undaunted.

"Same dough," was the reply.

In the spirit of being helpful, Jim told the clerk that they had been unable to locate the bakery's telephone number. Perhaps the telephone company had made a mistake in the listing?

"No mistake," the clerk said. "It's listed on the bag."

"On the bag?" Jim inquired.

"Right there," she said, indicating the telephone number, which was, indeed, listed on the paper bread bag containing the hot Italian loaves.

"But we didn't have a bag," Jim reasonably pointed out.

"Well," she shrugged, "you got one now."

The Italian bread from Pirecca's looked and tasted homemade. The rounds were hand-shaped, slightly irregular, without a slit on top and with no glaze. The ingredients were flour, salt, water and yeast. There were no dough enhancers or preservatives. The loaves were baked on a sheet pan, six to a pan. The bread had to be eaten on the day it was baked. By the second day it would taste slightly stale. Of course, it did not last till the second day. It was an unpretentious bread that was more satisfying to eat than to look at. It was easy to eat an entire loaf at a single sitting. A very good bread, we all decided as we picked the crumbs off the cutting board and ate them too.

The following day we traveled thirty-five miles north of Schenectady to visit a bakery which Henry had read about in one of his cookbooks. It was noted for its use of the latest developments in bread-baking technology. The bread was baked in extremely expensive, imported French ovens equipped with tile-floored decks and a steam injection apparatus. The loaves, after rising in wicker baskets, were inverted onto conveyor belts, slashed, moved into the ovens, and baked at 500 degrees. Besides doing a booming local business, the bakery weekly delivered around 3500 loaves to New York City.

We were prepared to be impressed. The manager-on-duty graciously gave us a tour of the bakery, which we found gratifyingly floury. The bakers, themselves well dusted with flour, took pride in their product and in their own skills. That particular morning a huge and hearty cinnamon-raisin loaf was just coming out of the ovens and the farmbread was going in. There was a fine array of fresh breads in the display case in the front of the bakery, including French, semolina, and whole wheat. At the conclusion of our tour we bought several loaves and the manager gave us a complimentary coffee mug. On our way back to Scotia we broke off hunks of the bread to taste, but having been informed by the store manager that the bread was actually baked so that it would be best on the second day, we kept most of the loaves whole for eating the following day.

Without a doubt, the loaves had beautiful sheen, intricate shape, thick-crusted character, and dense interior integrity. But, for me, eating them bore a remarkable similarity to the experience of viewing the abstract paintings of an avant-garde artist who is the current darling of the art community: After a few minutes of dutiful admiration, I sneak off to look at the landscapes.

So it was with the bread from the impressive new-age bakery. The next day we were back at Pirecca's for more of their "same dough" bread. And it didn't especially matter that the clerk was sullen, the hours were unposted, the telephone number was unlisted, and the bread had to be eaten on the same day.

Here at The Orange Blossom, we have found ourselves gradually gravitating more and more toward Pirecca's "same dough" philosophy. A few simple ingredients can be combined in a variety of ways to create satisfaction for the body, sustenance for the spirit, and pleasure for the imagination. We discovered, for example, that our sweet dough could be used for sticky buns, cinnamon rolls, coffee cake, even cake doughnuts.... And Moravian coffee bread dough could also make excellent hamburger buns.

Whenever I begin to lose my way in the maze of a complex Price Chopper culture, whenever I feel dazed and dazzled by the precise pronouncements of the New Age Bakery path to success, I find myself silently repeating the Pirecca mantra: *Same Dough, Same Dough....* It clears the fog, opens the mind, makes me smile, and, most of all, lets me see that life can be simple and still be good.

ORANGE BLOSSOM ITALIAN BREAD

8-8½ cups bread flour
1½ tablespoons salt
1½ tablespoons sugar
1½ tablespoons yeast

2 tablespoons vegetable
  shortening
3 cups warm water (100
  degrees)

Stir yeast into warm water and set aside. In a large mixing bowl, combine the flour, salt and sugar. Cut in the shortening till it resembles a fine meal. Make a well in the center and stir in the water and yeast. Continue stirring until all flour is incorporated and stirring becomes difficult. Place dough on a lightly floured surface and knead until smooth and elastic, about 10 minutes. Place in a lightly oiled bowl, cover with plastic wrap and then a kitchen towel. Let rise till dough has tripled in volume. Deflate and divide into three equal pieces. Shape into rounds and place on a parchment paper lined sheet pan. Cover lightly with plastic wrap and let rise until double in volume. Gently remove plastic and using a razor or a very sharp knife, make a shallow cut down the center of each loaf and then one on each side of center, being careful not to deflate dough. Bake in a 425 degree oven for approximately 40 minutes, covering with aluminum foil after bread is well browned. Cool on a wire rack.

PIZZA BREAD

This is fun and easy to make once you have the Italian bread dough. It's even good for breakfast.

1 piece of Italian bread
  dough, ready for baking

thick home-made or canned
  pizza sauce
Parmesan cheese

On a floured surface roll dough into a large rectangle about ¼ inch thick. Place on a lightly oiled sheet pan and spread on a thick layer of pizza sauce. Sprinkle over an even layer of grated Parmesan cheese. Cover loosely with an aluminum foil tent that will be high enough not to touch bread when fully risen. Let rise in a warm place until double in volume (the same amount of time as the Italian bread). Bake in a 425 degree oven along with bread and remove when crust is crisp and golden brown.

SEASONED GARLIC CROUTONS

1 loaf Italian bread
½ cup olive oil
1 teaspoon garlic powder
½ teaspoon onion powder
½ teaspoon paprika

1 teaspoon Italian seasoning
½ teaspoon salt
¼ teaspoon black pepper
⅛ teaspoon cayenne pepper

Cut enough bread into large cubes to obtain 4 cups. Place cubed bread in a single layer on a sheet pan and leave overnight at room temperature to harden. Combine the seasonings. In a large skillet heat ¼ cup olive oil, add 2 cups bread cubes and cook, stirring constantly until the oil is absorbed and the croutons are lightly browned. Sprinkle over ¼ of the seasonings and toss. Add more seasoning to taste. Place the croutons on a sheet pan. Repeat this process with the remaining 2 cups of bread cubes and place on sheet pan. Place pan in a 400 degree oven and bake until the croutons are well browned and crisp. Cool and store in an air-tight container at room temperature.

POTATO ROLLS

Perfect burger buns.

1½ cups peeled and diced
  potatoes
1 cup water
1 package dry yeast

6 tablespoons butter
1½ teaspoons salt
1 egg, beaten
4 cups all-purpose flour

Place potatoes in a saucepan, add 1 cup of water and bring to the boil. Cover and simmer over low heat until potatoes are tender. Drain, reserving the potato water. Puree the hot potatoes in an electric mixer. Beat in 6 tablespoons of butter, salt, and ½ cup of potato water. Cool ¼ cup of potato water (adding tap water if there is not enough left) to 110 degrees and stir in the yeast. When potato mixture has cooled (110 degrees), beat in yeast mixture. Beat in the egg and then the flour one cup at a time. Knead until dough is smooth and elastic (it will still be somewhat sticky). Place dough in a large, lightly oiled bowl. Cover with plastic wrap and then a kitchen towel. Let rise in a warm place until triple in volume. On a lightly floured surface divide dough into 12 equal pieces. Shape into rounds and then flatten into circles. Place circles on a lightly oiled sheet pan and flatten again. Cover with plastic wrap and let rise until double in a warm place. Remove the plastic and bake in a 375 degree oven until lightly browned and rolls sound hollow when lightly tapped underneath.

LETHA'S WAY WITH VEGETABLES

She wore "teacher's shoes," the old-fashioned, lace-up, dull-black leather sort with pinpoint-sized breathing holes and thick two-inch heels. Every teacher I was subjected to during my five years at Washington Elementary School in Shelby, North Carolina had worn shoes exactly like hers. Mrs. Moser, Mrs. Eskridge, Mrs. Bean—they all wore them. Like her, too, they had short tightly-curled blue-grey hair and they dressed in grey or olive green suits with severe lines and narrow lapels. They carried wooden rulers which they slapped against their open palms to punctuate pronouncements as they patrolled the aisles, the oiled floorboards creaking noisily beneath their sturdily shod feet in an otherwise breathtakingly quiet room.

Though I never saw her carrying a ruler, she looked in every other regard, when I first met her, like one of my elementary school teachers. Her name was Letha, and she was, in fact, a teacher. After attending the North Carolina Normal Institute for Women during the mid-1920's, she taught in a variety of small communities scattered across southwestern North Carolina. She lived in teacherages or boarded in private homes. When at the age of 50 she married my father, nearly a year to the date after he became a widower, she was what people called a real old maid.

They made the least likely couple one could imagine—my father with his seventh-grade education, his abiding fondness for Wild Turkey, and his deep affinity for barroom brawls; and Letha, who faithfully attended Central Methodist Church evening book-circle meetings, baked casseroles for the sick, the elderly, and the grieving, and devoted more than 40 years of her life to educating other people's children.

As a child on the edge of adolescence, I did not compile a list of differences in personality and background which set the two adults in my world on either side of a great chasm, but I marveled over the fact that Letha had come into our chaotic lives; and I could not for the life of me understand why she had chosen to give up what I considered to be a blissfully simple, neat, and ordered existence, when all she got in return was a tangled present and an uncertain future with us.

Little by little she effected changes in the way we lived. Not so slowly she shed the olive-green suits and the teacher's shoes, in favor of delicate pumps and pretty pastels. She was unostentatiously fond of lovely things and over the years she furnished our home and our lives with them, so gradually that we hardly noticed.

After a considerable time she and my father established a routine together. The days for each of them were spent in the workplace, as she continued to teach school while he went into business for himself as a housebuilder. Late afternoons for Letha were devoted to cooking, while my father worked on his houseplans. After dinner, she would settle into an easy chair with papers to grade, letters to write, clothing to mend. Still wearing her pumps, she crossed her feet daintily at the ankles. My father, barefoot and wearing a strap undershirt, would arrange himself in a big Lazy-Boy on the opposite side of the lamp which they shared and spread a newspaper across his lap for the purpose of shucking corn and fresh crowder peas and snapping the pole beans Letha had bought that day at a local produce stand. He always made enthusiastic comments on how fresh the vegetables were, and Letha would always respond with a mention of which farmer's stand she had obtained the vegetables from. Often the stand would be located many convoluted miles down a series of country roads in the middle of nowhere.

I often accompanied Letha on these afternoon expeditions to acquire fresh vegetables, not knowing exactly why I was going along. Perhaps it was the ride through the rolling farmland that was so appealing, or maybe it was the picturesque quality of the produce stands themselves. Some of them were little more than shacks; others were sturdy concrete structures. All of them were open to the air, with a roof overhead that sheltered the vegetables and the buyer from the heat of the sun. The proprietors were usually elderly people, too old to work the farm any longer. There always seemed to be two or three small children about, dressed in overalls and running around barefoot and careless under their grandparents' tolerant but watchful eye.

Letha knew the owners of the various stands by name, and they knew her as well. Sometimes she carried on a brief conversation with them about the quality of the current season's crop, then she would begin making her selections from a bountiful quantity and variety of home-grown vegetables arranged in baskets, boxes, cartons, and crates. She chose carefully, never buying too much of any one thing at a time, always keeping in mind the fact that my father, though he would cheerfully eat virtually any vegetable under the sun the first time it appeared on the table, would NOT touch a leftover. Moreover he tended to grow morose if he had to sit at the same table with people who were eating them. Accepting this idiosyncrasy of my father's with her customary good grace, Letha made it her practice to buy and cook precisely the right amount. Looking back now after many a year of stuffing my refrigerator full of little plastic bowls of leftover vegetables, I cannot fathom how she accomplished such a feat. Perhaps the truth is that she could have prepared enough food for an army, and we would have left not a crumb, for she was a truly gifted cook.

Her way with fresh vegetables was to let them speak for themselves. She used black and white pepper, onion, and sweet butter liberally for flavoring, but she tended to be sparing with other seasonings. One thing that made her meals special was the sheer variety of simply prepared dishes she offered. There were always three or more vegetables of complementary color, texture, and taste and they were inevitably accompanied by fresh melon wedges, a plate of sliced ripe tomatoes, a dish of a neighbor's bread and butter pickles, and a basket of hot biscuits, angelflake rolls, or buttered cornbread. Whatever meat we ate was merely a garnish for the wonderful array of vegetables she set before us in pretty, colorful bowls on a table covered with a fresh, crisp cloth.

To this day on the rare occasions when I happen upon a genuine farmer's produce stand, I remember Letha and our amicable jaunts to those long-since-gone vegetable stands of Cleveland County. Though I haven't a photograph of her on one of those expeditions, I can see her well, dressed no longer in drab olive green and prim teacher's shoes, but wearing her pretty pastels and slender pumps as she wanders amongst baskets brimful of fresh crowder peas and silver queen corn, cantaloupe and big-boy tomatoes, deep green okra and bright yellow squash, Mull's Orchard peaches and fat pole beans, crisp green onions and leafy lettuce, fine textured new potatoes and huge cabbage heads, tall celery stalks and pure purple turnips—all the splendid produce of our good earth.

Our vegetable sandwiches at The Orange Blossom are, I hope, a reflection of Letha's way with God's bountiful gifts.

VEGGIE DELIGHT

The delight of this sandwich is dependent on the summer freshness of the cucumbers and tomatoes served on just baked Italian bread. A simple mayonnaise on the bread works well in the summer months when tomatoes are in their prime. Otherwise creamy Parmesan, balsamic vinaigrette, and buttermilk ranch dressings are excellent alternatives to the mayo. Spread the dressing of choice on the bread slices (except in the case of vinaigrette, which should be sprinkled over the top of the vegetables) and top with the following:

thin slices of Swiss cheese　　**fresh red pepper slices**
tomato slices　　　　　　　　　**alfalfa sprouts**
cucumber slices　　　　　　　　**optional: 3 strips of crisply**
red onion slices　　　　　　　　　　**cooked bacon**
avocado slices　　　　　　　　　**leaf lettuce**

BROCCOLI SUPREME

This is a hot and hearty sandwich, satisfying to vegetarians and meat-eaters alike. First toast thick slices of Italian bread on one side, then spread the untoasted side with mustard-horseradish dressing, and place, dressing side up, on broiler pan. Meanwhile heat frozen broccoli florets on high power in microwave until hot but still crisp (about 2-3 minutes). Place heated broccoli florets on bread and top with a liberal amount of grated cheddar cheese. Also sprinkle cheddar on the slice of bread that will be used to top the sandwich. Toast under the broiler until the cheese is melted and bubbly. Remove. Over the broccoli florets arrange slices of red onion, fresh red pepper strips, and alfalfa sprouts. Cover with the top slice of cheese toast and serve hot.

frozen broccoli florets
mustard-horseradish
   dressing*
grated cheddar cheese

red onion slices
fresh red pepper slices
alfalfa sprouts

*For those who are not fond of horseradish, creamy Parmesan or buttermilk ranch dressing will also work well. See sandwich dressings and spreads, pages 86 and 87.

GREEK SALAD SANDWICH

Perfect for a summer beach hike; the salt in the olives and feta cheese replenishes the salt lost from sweating, and the lemon juice cuts the salt tang left in the mouth after an ocean swim.

1¼ cups roma tomatoes, cut
   into eighths
4 cups ruby lettuce, torn
   into bite size pieces
½ cup diced green pepper
¾ cup finely diced, peeled
   cucumbers

¼ cup halved and pitted
   Greek olives
¼ cup thinly sliced red onion
½ cup feta cheese, broken
   into chunks
lemon-garlic vinaigrette
   (see recipe page 86)
4 rounds of pita bread

Combine the salad ingredients in a large bowl. Shake the dressing ingredients to blend in a closed container, pour over the salad, and toss thoroughly. Cut pita bread rounds in half and stuff salad in pockets.

THE ZUCCHINI GRIN

With summer in full swing and vegetables from the garden coming in, it's a perfect time for making this garden-fresh sandwich.

1 whole medium to large zucchini, scrubbed to remove grit and cut lengthwise into ¼ inch thick slices
butter
salt and pepper
coarsely chopped parsley
lemon juice
red onion slices
tomato slices

grated white cheddar and Muenster cheese, evenly mixed
creamy Parmesan dressing (see recipe page 86)
crisp bacon slices
cucumber slices
sprouts
leaf lettuce, washed and dried
thick slices of Italian bread

Heat butter in a skillet. Sauté the zucchini slices briefly on each side, liberally peppering and lightly salting before and after turning. Drain on paper towels. Sprinkle with lemon juice. Toast Italian bread slices on one side under the broiler. Spread creamy Parmesan on the untoasted side of bread and place the zucchini slices on top, then cover both slices of bread with grated cheese and again place under the broiler. When the cheese is bubbly and lightly browned, remove from the broiler. Place all the vegetables and hot bacon on one slice of bread, then top with the remaining slice.

HUMMUS-IS-AMUNG-US

I used to make hummus when our son was very young and didn't like raw vegetables. What he *did* like was huge earth-moving equipment. So I made hummus for him, and he and I tacitly agreed that it was the earth. I cut up green pepper strips, which became steam shovels; celery became bulldozers, carrots were cranes, and pita bread pieces served as caterpillars. Whenever I would make this dish, I would call out loudly, "Hummus-is-amung-us," and three-year old Henry would come running, shouting gleefully, "Have you got my steam shovels ready?"

HUMMUS

2 garlic cloves
1 15-ounce can garbanzo
   beans, drained and
   rinsed
⅓ cup tahini (ground sesame
   seeds)

1 tablespoon plus 2
   teaspoons lemon juice
¼ cup water
⅛ teaspoon cayenne
⅛ teaspoon white pepper
½ teaspoon salt
½ teaspoon paprika

Puree garlic in a food processor. Add garbanzo beans, tahini, and lemon juice and blend. With machine running, slowly add the water and seasonings. When using the hummus in a sandwich, a thick consistency is preferable, but when using it as a dip, add another ¼ cup of water. Do not substitute cannelini beans for the garbanzos. The flavor is vapid. To make a sandwich, split a whole pita bread in half, stuff the pockets with hummus and add red pepper strips, cucumber slices and sprouts.

MOM'S PEPPERS AND PROVOLONE

Henry's brother Jim still remembers a special place his father took him after work when he was very young. It was a small smoke-filled tavern on a hill overlooking the city of Schenectady where immigrant workers would gather for beer and sandwiches of stewed peppers and provolone cheese on thick slices of fresh Italian bread. In later years, his mother would always make this for family gatherings.

ITALIAN STEWED PEPPERS

¼ cup olive oil
6 large green bell peppers
1 large sweet red pepper
½ large white onion, peeled
  and sliced

1 small can plum tomatoes
  plus juice
salt and pepper
provolone cheese slices
thick slices of Italian bread

Cut peppers in half lengthwise, core, and cut into large pieces. In a Dutch oven, heat olive oil until almost smoking. Add peppers and cook over medium heat for about 15 minutes, stirring occasionally. Add the onion; stir and cook for a few minutes. Add tomatoes, squeezing into small pieces with hands. Cover and cook on very low heat until peppers are tender, about ½ hour. Remove cover and evaporate excess liquid. Season with salt and pepper. Cool completely.

Cut thick slices of Italian bread and layer with peppers and thin slices of provolone cheese. Serve with lots of napkins and a cold beer.

THE CHIPOTLE CHOICE

2 slices fresh Italian bread
chipotle chile mayonnaise
  (see recipe page 87)
3 julienne strips each red,
  green, and yellow pepper
4 julienne strips fresh
  zucchini

5 washed leaves fresh
  spinach, julienned
1 teaspoon chopped fresh
  cilantro
sprinkle of fresh lime juice
mixture of grated Muenster
  and mild cheddar cheese

Toast bread slices on one side. Spread untoasted sides with chipotle
chile mayonnaise. Place peppers and zucchini on one slice of bread
and julienned spinach leaves on the other. Sprinkle chopped cilantro
and lime juice over both halves. Top each slice with cheese and place
under the broiler until cheese is bubbly and golden brown. Place two
halves together to make a whole. Slice diagonally in half.

BAGEL WORKS

*Any Southerner who has ever attended a gathering where food is served
cannot help but be acquainted with cream cheese and olive sandwiches,
which are usually made on dainty slices of white bread with the crusts
removed. At The Orange Blossom we make a heartier version of this Southern staple, which we serve on a toasted white or whole grain bagel.*

cream cheese, softened
sour cream
olive salad (see recipe page
  80)
crisp bacon

red onion slices
sprouts
leaf lettuce
tomato slices

In a mixer whip together desired amount of softened cream cheese
with a tablespoon or two of sour cream. Fold in olive salad to taste.
Spread the mixture on a toasted bagel half and top with bacon, red
onion, sprouts, lettuce and tomato. Cover with the remaining bagel
half and serve immediately.

MUFFALATA

This version is made with a variety of meats. We always used salami until one day when we happened to run out, we substituted pepperoni, and found that we liked it better. When using pepperoni slices, heat them first on a paper towel in the microwave to render the fat and crisp the meat. Place ingredients on the bread slice in the following order:

thin slices of provolone
    cheese
pepperoni or salami
thin slices of smoked turkey
olive salad (see recipe
    below)

red onion slices
tomato slices
balsamic vinaigrette (see
    recipe page 86)
leaf lettuce

Olive Salad
1 cup pimiento stuffed green
    olives, coarsely chopped
¼ cup finely chopped celery
2 teaspoons minced garlic
1 tablespoon chopped fresh
    parsley

1 tablespoon vegetable oil
1 teaspoon balsamic vinegar
¼ teaspoon dried oregano
¼ teaspoon red pepper
    flakes

Mix together all ingredients and refrigerate until serving.

SMOKED TURKEY TREAT

The most frequently ordered sandwich at the Orange Blossom, it is, indeed, a real treat. Spread mustard-horseradish dressing (see recipe page 87) on two thick slices of homemade Italian bread and stack the following ingredients high.

thin slices of smoked turkey
thin slices of Swiss cheese
3 crisply cooked slices of
    bacon per sandwich
sweet red pepper strips
    (jarred)

leaf lettuce
tomato slices
thin slices of red onion
sprouts

BLACKENED TUNA SANDWICH

A true Hatteras Island treat is freshly caught Gulf Stream tuna, dipped in butter and blackened seasonings, grilled, and served on toasted Italian bread with mayonnaise or balsamic vinaigrette.

**4 fresh tuna steaks,
    cut ¾ inch thick**

1 stick butter

Blackened seasonings
2 tablespoons paprika
1½ tablespoons salt
2 teaspoons onion powder
2 teaspoons garlic powder

1 tablespoon black pepper
1 teaspoon thyme
1 teaspoon oregano

**mayonnaise or balsamic
    vinaigrette**
thinly sliced red onion

leaf lettuce
sliced tomatoes

Melt the butter and stir in 2 tablespoons of the seasoning mix (save the rest in an air tight jar). Dip the tuna steaks in the seasoned butter and turn to coat on both sides. Chargrill or cook in a hot cast iron skillet, browning on both sides. Lightly toast thick slices of Italian bread and spread with mayonnaise (if using vinaigrette proceed to next step). Place lettuce over one slice, top with hot blackened tuna (if tuna was blackened in a skillet, pour some pan juices over tuna) and then top with sliced red onions and tomatoes (if using vinaigrette sprinkle over now). Cover with second slice of bread.

ROAST BEEF AND
PHILLY BAKE SANDWICHES

The absolute best way to eat homecooked rare roast beef is cold, on a hot summer day. The chilled beef should be cut in paper-thin slices, mounded on fresh-baked Italian bread, slathered with mustard-horseradish dressing or chipotle chile mayonnaise (see recipes page 87) and topped with a liberal quantity of red onion slices, juicy vine-ripened tomatoes, the highest quality Swiss cheese, and a big crisp leaf of romaine or ruby-red lettuce.

Unfortunately, it isn't always summer. During the remaining three seasons of the year, we like to eat our homecooked beef on a hot sandwich with a simple but delicious pepper, onion, and mushroom sauté.

Homecooked Beef
Using roast of preference, place meat on a sheet of aluminum foil in a large roasting pan and then into a preheated 400 degree oven. Cook until well browned and then cover loosely with aluminum foil. Continue cooking till done to individual preference. Test for doneness by inserting a long pronged fork into the center for 10 seconds. Remove fork and immediately touch bottom lip with the end of the fork. If prongs feel warm, the roast is medium rare. If cold, continue cooking and testing periodically. Cool completely before slicing.

Pepper, Onion, and
Mushroom Sauté
4 tablespoons vegetable oil
2 medium red bell peppers,
   cut into strips
1 large yellow onion, sliced
2 cloves garlic, minced

1 jalapeño, minced
2 cups mushrooms, rinsed,
   patted dry and sliced
salt and pepper

Sauté the peppers and onions in 2 tablespoons oil over high heat, stirring frequently, until the onions are translucent but still crisp. Add the garlic and jalapeño and season with salt and pepper. Cook briefly and set aside. Sauté mushrooms separately in remaining oil, seasoning with salt and pepper.

(Continued on next page)

(Roast Beef and Philly Bake Sandwiches, continued)

Compiling the Sandwich

sautéed onions and peppers
sautéed mushrooms
grated cheddar cheese
mustard-horseradish
    dressing or chipotle chile
    mayonnaise (see recipe
    page 87)

leaf lettuce
paper-thin slices of roast
    beef

Toast slices of Italian bread on one side under the broiler. Spread mustard-horseradish dressing or chipotle chile mayonnaise on the untoasted sides and return to the broiler. Lightly toast. Meanwhile, on a microwave safe plate, arrange a stack of roast beef slices to conform to the shape of the Italian bread slices. Top the beef with sautéed onions, peppers and mushrooms and a liberal sprinkling of grated cheddar cheese. Heat in the microwave on high power for about 2 minutes, or until the cheese is thoroughly melted and the beef is hot. Using a spatula, place the heated mixture on a toasted bread slice. Cover with leaf lettuce and top with the second slice of toast. Serve piping hot.

TUNA BURGER IN PARADISE

A real beach treat.

1 pound fresh, boneless,
    skinless tuna
1 tablespoon vegetable oil
¼ cup minced onion
1 teaspoon minced garlic
1 serrano or small jalapeño
    chile, minced
1 egg, lightly beaten

2 teaspoons soy sauce
¼ teaspoon black pepper
¼ teaspoon thyme
½ cup fresh breadcrumbs
4 potato rolls (see recipe
    page 71)
¼ cup melted butter

Cut tuna into large pieces and puree in food processor. Sauté onion, chile, and garlic in oil until wilted and add to tuna along with remaining ingredients. Process to combine. Remove from food processor and shape into four patties. Coat patties with oil and grill over hot charcoal. Cut potato rolls in half, brush with melted butter, and toast on grill. Serve burgers on toasted rolls with mayonnaise, lettuce, tomato and thinly sliced red onion.

CRAB CAKE SANDWICH
WITH A TOUCH OF HEAT

1 pound lump or backfin
crabmeat, picked through
to remove shell
2 scallions, finely chopped,
including a part of the
green tops
3 tablespoons finely chopped
sweet red pepper
1 serrano chile, finely
chopped (or two, when the
crab cake is to be eaten as
a sandwich)

2½ cups fresh breadcrumbs,
made from French bread
2 tablespoons mayonnaise
1 tablespoon Dijon mustard
1 tablespoon lemon juice
½ teaspoon salt
1 large egg, beaten
potato rolls (see recipe page
71)

Place crabmeat in a mixing bowl. Sauté scallions, red pepper and chile briefly in a little vegetable oil. Add to crab along with ½ cup of the breadcrumbs, mayonnaise, mustard, lemon juice, salt and egg. Mix gently and form into six round cakes. Roll the cakes in the remaining breadcrumbs. Sauté over moderate heat in a mixture of vegetable oil and butter (the oil keeps the butter from burning). Turn once. Cook until golden brown on both sides. Serve crab cakes on toasted potato rolls with mayonnaise, lettuce, tomato and thinly sliced red onion.

PURE CRAB CAKE SANDWICH

1 pound lump or backfin
 crabmeat, picked
 through to remove shells
1½ tablespoons flour
1 egg
3 tablespoons whipping
 cream
1 tablespoon minced parsley
2 teaspoons Dijon mustard
¼ teaspoon cayenne

¼ teaspoon hot pepper sauce
½ teaspoon salt
⅛ teaspoon pepper
2 cups fresh breadcrumbs,
 made from French bread
potato rolls (see recipe page
 71)
light and lemony tartar
 sauce (see recipe page
 88)

Place crabmeat in a mixing bowl. In another small bowl, beat the egg
and flour and then beat in the cream and seasonings. Add egg and
cream mixture to the crabmeat and mix gently. Form into six round
cakes and roll in breadcrumbs. Sauté in a mixture of ½ butter, ½ vegetable oil over moderate heat, turning once, until golden brown on
both sides. Serve on toasted potato rolls with light and lemony tartar
sauce.

FRESH FLOUNDER SANDWICH
WITH JALAPEÑO TARTAR SAUCE

1 pound flounder filets
1½ cups cornmeal
½ teaspoon salt
¼ teaspoon cayenne pepper
1 egg, beaten
4 tablespoons milk

French bread
jalapeño tartar sauce (see
 recipe page 88)
green leaf lettuce and sliced
 tomato

Combine the cornmeal, salt and cayenne in a flat dish. Mix together
the egg and milk. Dip filets one at a time in the egg mixture, dredge in
cornmeal and fry in hot oil skin side down until brown underneath.
Turn and cook until done. Drain on paper towels. Warm the loaf of
French bread, cut in half lengthwise and remove some of the interior.
Spread with jalapeño tartar sauce and top with flounder, lettuce and
sliced tomatoes.

BALSAMIC VINAIGRETTE

1 cup olive oil
6 tablespoons balsamic
    vinegar
1 teaspoon salt

½ teaspoon black pepper
1 small clove of garlic,
    peeled
dash of cayenne pepper

Mince garlic in salt and combine with other ingredients in a small mixing bowl. Whisk together to emulsify.

LEMON-GARLIC VINAIGRETTE

2 tablespoons lemon juice
½ teaspoon minced garlic
¼ cup olive oil

¼ teaspoon oregano
¼ teaspoon salt

Shake the dressing ingredients to blend in a closed container.

CREAMY PARMESAN DRESSING

1¼ cups mayonnaise
⅓ cup red wine vinegar
½ cup grated Parmesan
    cheese

1½ teaspoons minced garlic
¾ teaspoon black pepper
½ teaspoon salt
dash of hot sauce

Combine all ingredients in a bowl and mix well. Refrigerate until serving.

CREAMY MUSTARD DRESSING

2 large eggs (or equivalent
    amount egg beaters)
2 cups vegetable oil
6 tablespoons vinegar
1 teaspoon minced garlic
1 tablespoon yellow mustard
    (ballpark style, not Dijon)

1 tablespoon minced fresh
    parsley
1½ teaspoons dried oregano
1 teaspoon salt
½ teaspoon black pepper

Place the eggs in a food processor and with the motor running add the oil in a slow steady stream until thick. Add remaining ingredients and combine.

MUSTARD-HORSERADISH
SANDWICH SPREAD

1 cup mayonnaise
4 teaspoons Dijonnaise
    mustard
1½ teaspoons cider vinegar

1 teaspoon horseradish
¼ teaspoon sugar
⅛ teaspoon black pepper
⅛ teaspoon dried dill

In a mixing bowl, whisk together ingredients and refrigerate until serving.

CHIPOTLE CHILE MAYONNAISE

1 cup mayonnaise
1 canned chipotle chile in
    adobo sauce

juice of ½ lemon
1½ teaspoons finely minced
    garlic

Combine ingredients in food processor and blend to a fine puree.

LIGHT TARTAR SAUCE

1 cup mayonnaise
1 scallion, minced, including
    part of the green top
1 tablespoon parsley
¼ cup finely chopped pickled
    green tomato or dill pickle

¼ teaspoon finely minced
    garlic
1½ teaspoons horseradish
1 teaspoon Dijon mustard
⅛ teaspoon pepper
juice of one lemon

Blend all ingredients and refrigerate.

JALAPEÑO TARTAR SAUCE

1 egg (or substitute the
    equivalent of egg beaters)
1 clove garlic, minced
1 small jalapeño, minced
¾ cup vegetable oil
1 tablespoon *fresh* lime juice
½ teaspoon salt

1 tablespoon minced red
    onion
1 tablespoon chopped
    parsley
1 tablespoon minced sweet
    pickle
2 teaspoons Dijon mustard

Blend together egg, garlic, chile and salt in a food processor. With the machine running, gradually add the oil until thick. Blend in lime juice. Remove to a bowl and stir in the red onion, parsley, pickle and mustard.

Pizzas

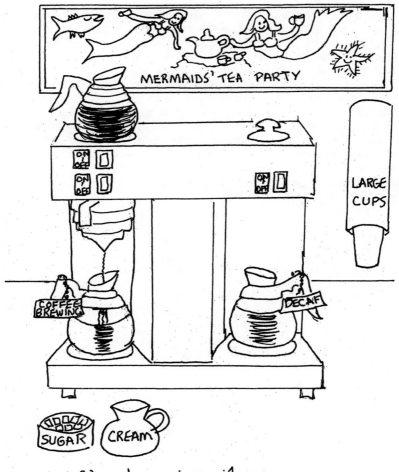

We're brewing it as
fast as we can.

ORANGE BLOSSOM DEEP-DISH PIZZA

We like to make pizza from the ingredients we happen to have on hand. Since we offer Mexican items on our lunch menu at the bakery, we naturally always have a lot of Mexican ingredients on hand. Therefore, although we enjoy Italian tomato sauce, we do not use one on our pizzas, but instead opt for our own red chile sauce. Mild red chilies, which can be found in dried form in the produce section of most supermarkets, give the pizza a subtly distinctive flavor, and they make for a smoother sauce, without the slightly raw taste of the traditional pizza sauce.

Coming up with just the right combination of toppings for a particular pizza and arranging them in a discernible order is an especially creative and individualistic activity. In other words, the end product is a result of a series of mistakes, which is how a great many recipes are developed, including our zucchini and mushroom pizza. One morning when it was especially hectic in the bakery, Ruth was assigned the task of making four different pizzas to put in the case. Henry had rattled off the names before dashing out of the kitchen to buy some forgotten but necessary item at Conner's Supermarket. Diligently Ruth rolled out her crusts and placed the appropriate toppings on three pizzas, but for the life of her, she couldn't remember what was supposed to be on the fourth: zucchini and something.

Jeannie and I weren't much help. The only thing we felt certain of was that there were mushrooms and that the zucchini should be grated rather than diced. Ruth spread red chile sauce over the pizza crust and put the grated cheese, zucchini and mushrooms over all. At that moment Henry returned from his errand. "What's that?" he said, peering at the unbaked pizza.

"Zucchini and mushroom pizza?" Ruth said.

"It doesn't get red chile sauce; it gets fresh, sliced tomatoes," Henry said. "The red chile sauce is too heavy."

We had to bake it anyway, since it couldn't be undone. It turned out to be far better with the red chile sauce than with the fresh tomatoes, so we've made it that way ever since.

ORANGE BLOSSOM DEEP DISH PIZZA

This recipe makes enough dough for a 15 inch diameter crust which is about ¾ inch thick when fully baked.

The Crust
1½ cups warm water
   (110 degrees)
2 tablespoons oil
1 package dry yeast

pinch of sugar
4 cups bread flour
1½ teaspoons salt

Combine the water and oil in a small bowl. Stir in the yeast and sugar and set aside until the mixture bubbles. In a large bowl, mix together the flour and salt and stir in the yeast mixture. When well combined, turn the dough out onto a lightly floured surface and knead until smooth and elastic (about 10 minutes). Place dough in a large, lightly oiled bowl. Cover the bowl with plastic wrap and then with a kitchen towel. Set aside in a warm place until triple in volume (about 1 hour).

CRUSTY GARLIC-PARMESAN BREAD STICKS

dough for 15 inch pizza
1 stick of butter, melted
garlic salt

grated Parmesan cheese
paprika

After the dough has gone through its first rise, cut it into two equal portions. Pour melted butter onto a 17½ x 12½ inch half-sheet pan. On a lightly floured surface, roll one piece of dough (second piece can be frozen for future use or made into a 12 inch pizza) into a 10 x 12 inch rectangle. Cut dough into 12-16 pieces 10 inches long and about ½ inch wide. Place strips side by side on sheet pan, turning to coat thoroughly in butter. Sprinkle liberally with garlic salt and then Parmesan cheese. Turn again and repeat on other side. Dust with paprika. Set aside in a warm place to proof ½ hour. Bake in a 425 degree oven until golden brown and crusty (about 20 minutes). Cool on a wire rack.

BREAKFAST PIZZA

1 pound hot Italian sausage,
  casings removed,
  browned well, and
  drained
½ large white onion, sliced
1 sweet red pepper, diced
chopped jalapeño

shredded cheese
10 beaten eggs, seasoned
  with salt and pepper
1 15 inch pizza crust, made
  with all-purpose flour
black pepper

Sauté onion, jalapeño, and red pepper in hot oil. Add sausage and combine well. Cover pizza crust with shredded cheese. Evenly distribute sausage mixture over cheese. Pour over eggs and sprinkle lightly with additional cheese. Bake in 425 degree oven until crust is golden brown and eggs are set.

WESTERN BREAKFAST PIZZA

½ medium white onion,
  diced
½ large red pepper, diced
1 jalapeño, minced
diced ham
sautéed mushrooms

1 15 inch pizza crust, made
  with all-purpose flour
shredded pizza cheese
10 beaten eggs, seasoned
  with salt and pepper
black pepper

Sauté onion, red pepper and jalapeño in hot oil until soft. Add diced ham and brown well. Cover crust with cheese. Distribute ham mixture and mushrooms evenly over cheese. Pour over eggs and lightly sprinkle over more cheese. Bake in a 425 degree oven for 20-25 minutes.

SPINACH, MUSHROOM, SCALLION, JALAPEÑO AND BACON PIZZA

dough for 15 inch pizza (see recipe page 91)
⅔ cup red chile sauce (see recipe page 112)
3 cups sliced fresh mushrooms, sautéed in 2 tablespoons olive oil
1 large scallion, finely chopped (white and green part)
1 cup spinach filling (see recipe page 102)

1 jalapeño, minced
4 slices bacon, cooked crisp and finely chopped (optional)
⅓ pound grated mild white cheddar cheese
⅓ pound grated Muenster cheese
⅓ pound grated mozzarella cheese

Preheat oven to 425 degrees. On a lightly floured surface, roll dough into a circle. Lightly flour the top and fold the dough into quarters (folding in half and then in half again). Lightly oil a 15 inch deep dish baking pan. Place the dough in the pan and unfold, pressing with fingers to distribute it evenly to the edge. Spoon red chile sauce evenly over the dough. Mix together the three cheeses and reserving 1 cup, sprinkle the rest evenly over the sauce. Distribute spinach and mushrooms evenly over the cheese. Combine the scallions, jalapeño and bacon and sprinkle over the top. Sprinkle the reserved cheese over all and set pan aside for 10 minutes. Place pan on the lowest shelf of oven and bake until the bottom of crust is golden brown (about 25 minutes). Remove the pizza from the pan and cool on a wire rack for 10 minutes. Cut into 8 pieces.

SWEET PEPPER, BASIL AND CHEESE PIZZA

4 sweet red peppers
¼ cup olive oil
½ teaspoon salt
2 serrano chilies, diced
dough for 15 inch pizza
    crust (see recipe page 91)
⅔ cup red chile sauce (see
    recipe page 112)

1 bunch fresh basil
⅓ pound grated mild white
    cheddar cheese
⅓ pound grated Muenster
    cheese
⅓ pound grated mozzarella
    cheese

Preheat oven to 425 degrees. Wash the red peppers, remove the stems and seeds and cut into large pieces. Combine in a Dutch oven with the olive oil and salt. Cover and bake for one hour or until peppers are softened. Remove from oven, cool, and reserve. On a lightly floured surface, roll the dough into a circle. Lightly flour the top and fold the dough into quarters (folding in half and then in half again). Lightly oil a 15 inch deep dish pizza pan. Place the dough in the pan and unfold, pressing with your fingers to distribute it evenly to the edge. Spoon the red chile sauce evenly over the dough. Mix together the three cheeses and, reserving 1 cup, sprinkle evenly over the sauce. Distribute the reserved red peppers and serrano chilies over the cheese. Remove the basil leaves from the stems, wash, dry and cut into strips. Mix together the basil strips and reserved cheese. Sprinkle evenly over the top. Set pan aside for 15 minutes. Place pan on the lowest shelf of oven and bake for 10 minutes. Cover pan with aluminum foil and continue baking until the bottom of the crust is golden brown (about 15 minutes more). Remove pizza from the pan and cool on a wire rack for 5 minutes. Cut into 8 pieces.

BLACK BEAN, PEPPER, SCALLION, JALAPEÑO AND BACON PIZZA

dough for 15 inch pizza (see recipe page 91)
⅔ cup red chile sauce (see recipe page 112)
1 cup cooked black beans, drained (see recipe page 108)
2 tablespoons olive oil
1 cup diced white onion
½ cup diced sweet red pepper
½ cup diced green bell pepper

1½ teaspoons minced garlic
¼ teaspoon dried thyme
1 fresh jalapeño, minced
5 slices bacon, cooked crisp and finely chopped
⅓ pound grated mild white cheddar cheese
⅓ pound grated Muenster cheese
⅓ pound grated mozzarella cheese

Preheat oven to 425 degrees. In a large skillet, sauté the onion, peppers, garlic, jalapeño, and thyme in olive oil until barely tender. Cool and mix together with black beans. Reserve. On a lightly floured surface, roll dough into a circle. Lightly flour the top and fold dough into quarters (folding in half and then in half again). Lightly oil a 15 inch deep dish baking pan. Place the dough in the pan and unfold, pressing with fingers to distribute it evenly to the edge. Spoon red chile sauce evenly over the dough. Mix together the three cheeses and reserving 1 cup, sprinkle the rest evenly over the sauce. Distribute the reserved bean mixture evenly over the cheese. Sprinkle over the bacon and then the reserved cheese. Set aside for 10 minutes. Place the pan on the lowest shelf of oven and bake until the bottom of crust is golden brown (about 25 minutes). Remove pizza from pan and cool on a wire rack for 10 minutes. Cut into 8 pieces.

ITALIAN SAUSAGE AND PEPPER PIZZA

To make this pizza, follow the directions for the peppers and cheese pizza (see recipe page 98) using less peppers in the topping and adding some sausage made according to the following recipe.

ITALIAN SAUSAGE

1 pound ground turkey (much less fat, same taste) or pork
2 teaspoons minced garlic
2 teaspoons fennel seeds
2 teaspoons Italian seasoning
1 teaspoon onion powder
1 teaspoon hot paprika
1 teaspoon crushed red pepper flakes
1 teaspoon salt
¼ teaspoon black pepper
2 tablespoons dry red wine

Combine all ingredients in a bowl and mix well. To use as a pizza topping, pinch off bite-size pieces and fry in a skillet, in a little vegetable oil, browning well on both sides.

ZUCCHINI AND MUSHROOM PIZZA

dough for 15 inch pizza (see recipe page 91)
⅔ cup red chile sauce (see recipe page 112)
3 cups sliced fresh mushrooms, sautéed in 2 tablespoons olive oil
1 medium zucchini, washed, scrubbed, and grated
red pepper flakes
½ pound grated Muenster cheese
½ pound grated mild white cheddar cheese

Preheat oven to 425 degrees. On a lightly floured surface, roll dough into a circle. Lightly flour the top and fold the dough into quarters (folding in half and then in half again). Lightly oil a 15 inch deep dish pizza pan. Place the dough in the pan and unfold, pressing with your fingers to distribute it evenly to the edge. Spoon red chile sauce evenly over the dough. Mix together the two cheeses and reserving 1 cup, sprinkle the rest evenly over the sauce. Distribute the zucchini evenly over the cheese and then do the same with the mushrooms. Sprinkle over red pepper flakes. Top with reserved cheese and set the pan aside for 10 minutes in a warm place. Place pan on the lowest shelf of oven and bake until the bottom is golden brown (about 25 minutes). Remove the pizza from the pan and cool on a wire rack for 10 minutes. Cut into 8 pieces.

TACO PIZZA

**dough for a 15 inch pizza
crust (see recipe page 91)**
**½ pound shredded Muenster
cheese**
**½ pound shredded mild
white cheddar cheese**

**quick salsa (see recipe page
110)**
**picadillo (see recipe page
106)**
**chile powder (pure), cumin,
oregano**

Preheat oven to 425 degrees. Lightly oil a 15 inch deep-dish pizza pan. On a lightly floured surface, roll the dough into a circle. Lightly flour the top and fold the dough into quarters (folding in half and then in half again). Place the dough in the pan and unfold, pressing with your fingers to distribute it evenly to the edge. Mix together the two cheeses and reserving 1 cup, sprinkle the rest evenly over the dough. Distribute the picadillo evenly over the cheese (you will have some left over). Place a colander in a mixing bowl and add the salsa to drain off the excess liquid (saving the liquid for another use). Distribute the salsa over the picadillo. Sprinkle on the reserved cheese. Sprinkle the top lightly with the chile powder, cumin and oregano. Set the pan aside for 15 minutes. Place the pan on the lowest shelf of the oven and bake for 10 minutes. Cover the pan loosely with a sheet of aluminum foil and bake for about 15 more minutes or until bottom crust is golden brown. Remove the pan from the oven and remove the pizza from the pan to cool briefly on a wire rack. Cut into 8 pieces.

THREE PEPPER AND CHEESE PIZZA

4 sweet red peppers
4 fresh Anaheim chilies
¼ cup olive oil
½ teaspoon salt
dough for 15 inch pizza
   crust (see recipe page 91)
⅔ cup red chile sauce (see
   recipe page 112)

⅓ pound grated mild white
   cheddar cheese
⅓ pound grated Muenster
   cheese
⅓ pound grated mozzarella
   cheese
1 fresh jalapeño, minced

Preheat oven to 425 degrees. Wash peppers, peel, seed, and cut into chunks. Combine in Dutch oven with olive oil and salt. Cover and bake in a 400 degree oven for 1 hour. Remove from oven; cool and reserve. On a lightly floured surface, roll the dough into a circle. Lightly flour the top and fold the dough into quarters (folding in half and then in half again). Lightly oil a 15 inch deep dish pizza pan. Place the dough in the pan and unfold, pressing with fingers to distribute it evenly to the edge. Spoon red chile sauce evenly over the dough. Mix together the three cheeses and reserving 1 cup, sprinkle the rest evenly over the sauce. Distribute the reserved peppers over the cheese (there will be some peppers left over), alternating the red and green colors. Sprinkle on the minced jalapeño and then the reserved cheese. Set pan aside for 10 minutes. Place pan on the lowest shelf of oven and bake until the bottom crust is golden brown (about 25 minutes). Remove pizza from the pan and cool on a wire rack for 10 minutes. Cut into 8 pieces.

Mexican Specialties

Our blue stove
keeps us warm
on winter days-

SEAFOOD ENCHILADAS

A delicious way to combine shrimp and crabmeat.

How to Boil Shrimp
The simplest way to prepare shrimp is to boil them. Straightforward enough, but it's surprising how many folks manage to botch this. To avoid ending up with tasteless rubbery balls that bounce right off your plate, try the following method.

Per pound of shrimp, use one quart of water. Bring the water to a rapid boil. For peeled and deveined shrimp, use one tablespoon of salt per pound of shrimp. For shrimp in their shells, use two tablespoons of salt per pound of shrimp. Add the proper amount of salt and then the shrimp to the boiling water. Return to the boil and cook for three to four minutes over medium heat, the length of time depending on the size of the shrimp. When the shrimp curl, they're done. Drain immediately in a colander and rinse under cold water to stop the cooking process.

Shrimp Filling
1¼ pounds boiled medium size shrimp, peeled and deveined
1 tablespoon butter
¼ cup finely chopped scallions
¼ teaspoon salt
¼ teaspoon oregano
⅛ teaspoon cayenne pepper
⅛ teaspoon white pepper
¼ cup sour cream
4 ounces Monterey Jack cheese, shredded

Place shrimp in a mixing bowl. Sauté the scallions and seasonings in butter briefly to combine flavors. Pour scallion mixture over the shrimp and stir. Add the sour cream and cheese. Combine well and set aside.

Crab Filling
½ pound fresh lump crabmeat, picked through carefully to remove all shell and cartilage
½ pound cream cheese, softened
1 tablespoon butter
¼ cup finely chopped onion
3 ounces grated Monterey Jack cheese
⅓ cup cheese enchilada filling (see recipe page 102)

Sauté onion briefly in butter and combine with remaining ingredients. Set aside.

(Continued on next page)

100

(Seafood Enchiladas, continued)

Assembly and Baking (serves 6)

shrimp filling
crab filling
1½ cups white sauce (see
    recipe page 113)

12 corn tortillas
1½ cups grated Monterey
    Jack cheese
paprika

Spoon a thin layer of sauce in the bottom of an oven-proof, lightly oiled casserole. Place three tablespoons of filling down the center of each tortilla, filling 6 with the crab mixture and 6 with the shrimp mixture. Roll up and place seam side down in casserole dish. Spoon a layer of sauce over each enchilada and sprinkle Jack cheese over all. Dust lightly with paprika and bake in a 400 degree oven until golden brown and bubbly. Place one shrimp and one crab enchilada on each plate and serve with Spanish rice (see page108) and black beans (see page 108).

CHICKEN ENCHILADAS

A regular item on the Orange Blossom lunch menu. We have some customers who order this, once a week, each week that we are open.

1 pound cooked, boneless,
    skinless, chicken breast,
    chopped
1 tablespoon vegetable oil
½ cup diced onion
¼ pound cream cheese, cut
    into 4 pieces
⅓ cup half-and-half
¾ teaspoon salt

¼ teaspoon black pepper
white sauce (see recipe page
    113)
8 corn tortillas
½ pound grated mild, white
    cheddar or Monterey
    Jack cheese
paprika

In a large skillet, sauté the onions in vegetable oil until soft. Add the half-and-half, cream cheese, salt and pepper, and whisk over medium-low heat until smooth. Do not boil. Remove pan from the heat and add the chicken. In an oven-proof casserole, spoon in a thin layer of sauce. Divide the filling evenly down the centers of the tortillas, roll up and place seam side down in baking dish. Ladle 2 tablespoons of sauce over each tortilla, sprinkle with grated cheese, and dust with paprika. Bake in a 400 degree oven till brown and bubbly.

VEGETARIAN ENCHILADAS

Spinach Filling

2 packages frozen, chopped
   spinach, defrosted and
   squeezed dry
2 tablespoons butter

¼ cup minced onion
1½ teaspoons minced garlic
½ teaspoon salt
⅛ teaspoon black pepper

Place spinach in a mixing bowl. In a skillet, sauté onion and garlic in butter until soft, stir in salt and pepper, and pour over spinach. Mix well and reserve.

Cheese Filling

½ pound ricotta cheese
1 scallion, chopped
1 small jalapeño, chopped
½ teaspoon salt

¾ pound grated, mild, white
   cheddar or Monterey
   Jack cheese

Combine ingredients in a mixing bowl and set aside.

Final Assembly (to serve 4)

spinach filling
cheese filling
black beans (see recipe page
   108)
red chile sauce (see recipe
   page 112)

12 corn tortillas
2 cups grated mild, white
   cheddar or Monterey
   Jack cheese

Lightly oil a large casserole dish. For each enchilada, place about ⅓ cup of filling down the center of a corn tortilla, roll up, and place seam side down in casserole dish. Using this method, prepare four each: spinach, cheese, and black bean enchiladas. Ladle a thin layer of red chile sauce over all and top with grated cheese. Bake in a 400 degree oven till golden brown and bubbly. Place one spinach, one cheese and one black bean enchilada on each of four plates and serve with Spanish rice (recipe page 108).

CHILES RELLENOS

This is perhaps Henry's favorite New Mexican food. Though the basic recipe for a cheese-stuffed green chile has only a few ingredients, it is time-consuming to prepare, primarily because one must first remove the outer skin from the fresh Anaheim chilies called for. There are a variety of methods for peeling the chilies. Henry prefers to place them on a hot char-grill. When the underside is thoroughly blistered, turn and continue grilling until the chilies are blistered all around. Place the chilies in a plastic bag for a few minutes. Then peel the skin off and cool (when not grilling, use broiler in oven).

8 large Anaheim chilies	frying shortening
1 pound Monterey Jack cheese	green chile sauce (see recipe page 111)
beer batter (see recipe below)	2 cups grated Monterey Jack cheese

Prepare chilies for stuffing using the method given above. Cut an equal number of sticks of Monterey Jack cheese about ¾ inch in thickness and the same length as the chilies being used. At the tip of the chile (not the stem end), cut a small slit and push the cheese stick in to the stem. Press the chile gently to seal and continue the process until all the chilies are stuffed. Heat frying shortening to 375 degrees. Dip chilies in beer batter and deep fry until golden brown (a few at a time). Drain on paper towels. Place in an oiled casserole dish. Top each chile with green chile sauce, sprinkle with grated cheese, and bake in a 375 degree oven until melted and bubbly. Serve two chilies per person along with beans and rice for a delicious meatless meal.

Beer Batter

1⅓ cups flour	¼ teaspoon black pepper
2 egg yolks	1 cup flat beer (left open overnight)
1 tablespoon oil	
1 teaspoon salt	

Combine flour, egg yolks, oil, salt and pepper in a food processor. Blend 30 seconds and then with machine running, pour in enough beer to make a thick batter. Set aside for 30 minutes before using.

BEANS AND GREENS BURRITO

All good things come together in this popular lunch burrito at the Orange Blossom.

½ cup black beans (see recipe page 108)
⅓ cup sautéed spinach (see recipe page 102)
2 tablespoons salsa cruda (see recipe page 110)
2 teaspoons red chile sauce (see recipe page 112)
⅓ cup grated mild white cheddar or Monterey Jack cheese
8 inch flour tortillas

Spoon ½ cup black beans down the center of the flour tortilla. Evenly distribute spinach over the beans and top with salsa. Roll up the tortilla and place on a lightly oiled shallow baking pan. Spread 2 teaspoons of red chile sauce over the top and sprinkle with grated cheese. Bake in a 400 degree oven till very hot and crispy. Serve with Spanish rice.

BLACK BEAN TOSTADA

During our Mexican restaurant years, we would occasionally go to dinner in our own restaurant and, no matter what was on the menu, Michal would always order a black bean tostada and a beef fajita.

½ cup black beans (see recipe page 108)
⅓ cup shredded Monterey Jack cheese
1 tablespoon guacamole (see recipe page 112)
1½ teaspoons sour cream
⅓ cup shredded lettuce
1 tablespoon diced tomato
corn tortilla
vegetable oil

Fry tortilla in hot oil until crisp on both sides. Drain. Spoon ½ cup of black beans evenly over the top and sprinkle with grated cheese. Place in a baking pan and then in a 400 degree oven and bake until cheese is melted. Transfer tostada to a serving plate. Top with guacamole, sour cream, shredded lettuce, and diced tomato.

CHICKEN MOLÉ

Molé is a rich and complex Mexican sauce, made easy by the use of molé paste, imported from Mexico.

3 boneless, skinless, chicken breasts, cut in half
¼ pound butter
juice of ½ lemon
1 serrano chile, finely chopped
2 tablespoons vegetable oil
2 cups sliced onions
1 teaspoon garlic
½ teaspoon cinnamon

½ cup canned tomatoes, pureed
¼ cup peanut butter
¾ jar molé paste (Donna Maria preferred)
2 teaspoons sugar
1 teaspoon salt
¼ teaspoon pepper
3 cups chicken stock
sesame seeds
sour cream

Sauté chile briefly in butter, add lemon juice, pour over chicken, and marinate ½ hour. In a large heavy-bottomed pot, sauté the onions and garlic in vegetable oil until soft. Add the cinnamon, tomatoes, and peanut butter and cook a few minutes. Meanwhile, combine the molé paste, sugar, salt, pepper and 1 cup of chicken stock in a blender and puree. Add molé mixture to the onion mixture, along with remaining stock, and cook about 15 minutes, stirring occasionally. Over a hot charcoal fire, grill chicken breasts and place on serving dish. Coat each breast with molé sauce and sprinkle with sesame seeds. Serve with sour cream.

SKIRT STEAK FAJITAS

2½ pounds skirt steak (very flavorful and tender, but sometimes difficult to find; any tender cut of beef may be substituted)
½ cup soy sauce
2 tablespoons brown sugar
1 tablespoon lemon juice
½ teaspoon ground ginger
¼ teaspoon garlic powder
¼ teaspoon onion powder
¼ teaspoon red pepper flakes
2 tablespoons vegetable oil
1 cup sliced onions
1 cup sliced green pepper
salt and pepper

Prepare a hot charcoal grill. In a bowl, whisk together soy sauce, brown sugar, lemon juice, ginger, garlic powder, onion powder and red pepper flakes. Place meat in a non-aluminum pan and pour over marinade. Marinate for 30 minutes at room temperature. Meanwhile, in a skillet, sauté onions and green peppers in vegetable oil until wilted and season with salt and pepper. Grill steak medium rare and cut across the grain into wafer thin slices. Serve with hot flour tortillas, the sautéed onions and green peppers, guacamole (see recipe page 112), and salsa cruda (see recipe page 110).

PICADILLO

Picadillo means spiced ground meat. It is usually made with apples, cinnamon, raisins and a multitude of spices. However, the flavor of this version comes from the fiery and piquant serrano pepper, onions and fresh tomatoes. It is perfect when served in a soft taco shell with refried beans, lettuce, salsa, and sour cream.

¼ cup vegetable oil
2 pounds ground beef
1½ teaspoons garlic powder
1½ teaspoons salt
¼ teaspoon black pepper
1½ cups chopped onion
2 to 3 serrano peppers, finely chopped (jalapeños may be substituted)
1¼ cups fresh tomatoes, diced

Heat oil in a skillet. Add beef and brown, seasoning with garlic powder, salt and pepper. Drain off excess grease. Add onions and chilies and continue cooking and stirring until onions are translucent. Add fresh tomatoes and cook a few minutes more.

PINTO BEANS

First Day
3 cups dried pinto beans
12 cups water

1 teaspoon salt
¼ teaspoon black pepper

Place the beans at the top of a large sheet pan. While pulling the beans toward the other end of pan, examine carefully, and remove small rocks and grit. Place beans in a colander and rinse well. In a large pot, bring water to a boil, add the beans and bring back to the boil for 1 minute. Turn off heat, cover, and soak for 1 hour. Return to the boil and simmer until beans are tender (about 2½ hours). Season with salt and pepper.

Second Day Pinto Beans
3 cups cooked pinto beans
    plus cooking liquid
3 tablespoons vegetable oil

½ cup shredded mild white
    cheddar or Monterey
    Jack cheese
1 serrano chile, minced
    (optional)

Heat oil in a large cast iron skillet till almost smoking. Spoon in the beans, mashing well after each addition, into a smooth puree and adding enough liquid to make them soupy. Stir in cheese and chile. Serve immediately.

WELL-SEASONED PINTO BEANS

Flavorful and mildly spicy.

3½ cups dried pinto beans
7 cups water
1 whole jalapeño

1 onion, peeled and cut in half
1½ teaspoons salt
½ teaspoon black pepper

Place the beans at the top of a large sheet pan. While pulling the beans toward the other end of the pan, examine carefully, and remove small rocks and grit. Place beans in a colander and rinse well. In a large pot, bring water to a boil, add the beans and bring back to the boil for one minute. Turn off the heat, cover, and soak for 1 hour. Add onion and jalapeño and return to the boil. Partially cover and simmer until beans are tender (about 2½ hours). Season with salt and pepper.

FAT-FREE "REFRIED" BEANS

Same texture, great taste, no fat.

Prepare well-seasoned pinto beans and drain in colander, saving liquid. Place beans immediately in the bowl of an electric mixer and gradually add the reserved liquid, while beating into a smooth puree.

BLACK BEANS

3½ cups dried black beans
7 cups water
¾ cup finely chopped onion
1½ jalapeños, finely chopped

1 tablespoon minced garlic
1½ teaspoons cumin
1½ teaspoons salt
¼ teaspoon black pepper

Place the beans at the top of a large sheet pan. While pulling the beans toward the other end of the pan, examine carefully, and remove small rocks and grit. Place beans in a colander and rinse well. In a large pot, bring the water to a boil, add the beans and bring back to the boil for 1 minute. Turn off the heat, cover, and soak for 1 hour. Add the onion, jalapeño, garlic and cumin. Return to the boil, reduce heat, and simmer until the beans are tender (about 2½ hours). Season with salt and pepper.

SPANISH RICE

A classic recipe and very good with freshly made black beans and salsa.

1 tablespoon butter
2 tablespoons minced onion
2 tablespoons minced sweet
  red pepper
1 small clove of garlic, minced
1 cup parboiled long grain
  rice

2 cups hot chicken broth
2 tablespoons frozen green
  peas
2 tablespoons frozen corn
  kernels
1 teaspoon salt (less if using
  seasoned stock)

In an ovenproof saucepan, sauté the onion, red pepper and garlic in butter for a few minutes. Stir in the rice and the remaining ingredients. Bring to a boil, cover, and bake in a 350 degree oven until all the liquid is absorbed (about 25 minutes).

Salsas, Sauces, and Dips

Break Time
on
The Orange Blossom Swing

QUICK SALSA

When you are in a hurry.

1 10 ounce can Rotel diced
   tomatoes and green
   chilies, pureed in a food
   processor
1 tablespoon chopped fresh
   jalapeño

1 tablespoon minced
   cilantro
¼ teaspoon salt
¼ teaspoon garlic powder
¼ teaspoon onion powder
juice of ½ small lime

Combine ingredients.

SALSA CRUDA

1 tablespoon vegetable oil
¼ cup finely chopped white
   onion
1½ teaspoons minced garlic
2 cups diced fresh tomatoes
1½ cups canned crushed
   tomatoes
⅓ cup tomato puree

8 ounces canned diced green
   chilies
2 tablespoons finely
   chopped jalapeño
¾ teaspoon cumin
1½ teaspoons salt
½ teaspoon black pepper
water

Sauté the onions and garlic in vegetable oil until soft. Remove from heat and cool completely. In a large bowl combine the remaining ingredients, except water. Stir in the cooled onions and garlic and refrigerate until serving time. Stir in water before serving to obtain desired consistency. Serve with tortilla chips, baked or fried.

BLACK-EYED PEA SALSA

1 cup frozen black-eyed peas, cooked 5 minutes, drained, and rinsed under cold water

⅓ cup finely chopped celery heart

⅓ cup finely minced red onion

½ cup frozen corn kernels, defrosted

4 roma tomatoes, finely chopped (about 1¼ cups)

1 large fresh jalapeño, minced

1 cup tomato juice

2 tablespoons extra virgin olive oil

juice of ½ lime (or more to taste)

1 tablespoon balsamic vinaigrette (see recipe page 86)

1 tablespoon minced pickled jalapeño

1 tablespoon minced cilantro (or more to taste)

½ teaspoon salt

⅛ teaspoon black pepper

Combine ingredients and refrigerate.

GREEN CHILE SAUCE

2 tablespoons vegetable oil

¾ cup diced onion

1 teaspoon minced garlic

3 cups fresh tomatoes, cored and diced

½ cup tomato puree

8 ounces canned diced green chilies (mild)

¾ teaspoon salt

¼ teaspoon black pepper

¼ teaspoon ground coriander

Sauté onions and garlic until translucent. Add remaining ingredients and simmer gently for ½ hour.

RED CHILE SAUCE

2 dried New Mexico red
   chilies
2 cups boiling water
2 tablespoons vegetable oil
1½ teaspoons minced garlic
1 tablespoon flour

½ cup water
4 cups canned tomato sauce
1 teaspoon oregano
⅛ teaspoon hot sauce
⅛ teaspoon black pepper
½ cup water

Wash chilies and remove stems. Shake seeds into a fine sieve, rinse, and reserve. Tear chilies into pieces, place in a stainless steel bowl, and pour over boiling water. Cover and let chilies soak for 15 minutes. Drain in colander, saving soaking liquid. Place chilies in blender container and add enough soaking liquid to make a fine puree when blended. Reserve. In a large saucepan cook the garlic in oil briefly (do not brown), stir in flour and cook 1 minute. Whisk in water and bring to a boil. Add reserved chilies, chile seeds and remaining ingredients. Simmer, over low heat, partially covered for ½ hour.

GUACAMOLE

After trying every conceivable variation that we could think of, the following is our best recipe for guacamole: simple, garlicky and delicious. A few things to keep in mind when making guacamole: Always use Haas avocados that are dead ripe (skin will be black and fruit will be soft but not mushy). Make it the same day it will be eaten; guacamole does not keep well.

2 pounds mashed, ripe
   avocado pulp
¼ cup diced fresh jalapeños
2 teaspoons lemon juice

2 teaspoons lime juice
1-2 teaspoons salt
¼ teaspoon pepper
2 teaspoons minced garlic

Combine ingredients. Use immediately or refrigerate with plastic wrap, directly covering the surface (to avoid discoloration) until ready to use. Serve with tortilla chips or use as a sauce for a multitude of Mexican dishes (i.e. fajitas, tacos, burritos, huevos rancheros, etc.)

CHILE CON QUESO

Chile con queso is a smooth and creamy dip with a touch of fire that settles at the back of the throat. The cream soothes while the serranos stir up the appetite, a combination that guarantees that a person will keep on eating. It's delicious served as is with tortilla chips, and also makes an excellent sauce to use on burritos.

3 cups milk
3 cups half-and-half
8 ounces cream cheese, softened
½ cup cornstarch, dissolved in ¼ cup cold water
1 pound grated sharp cheddar cheese
¼ cup minced scallions, with tops

1 teaspoon minced garlic
2 tablespoons dry white wine
¾ cup diced mild green chilies
⅓ cup diced pimientos
4 tablespoons finely minced serrano chilies (hot)
1½ teaspoons salt
¼ teaspoon pepper

In a large heavy-bottomed pot, scald the milk and cream. Remove from the heat and whisk in the cream cheese. Return to moderate heat and whisk in the cornstarch mixture. Continue whisking to the boil. Cook over low heat for five minutes, stirring constantly. Remove from the heat and stir in the cheddar cheese. Combine wine, scallions and garlic in a non-aluminum pan and cook over moderate heat until most of the liquid has evaporated. Stir into the cheese mixture. Add remaining ingredients. Serve with tortilla chips.

WHITE SAUCE

2 tablespoons butter
3 tablespoons flour
2 cups half-and-half
½ teaspoon salt

⅛ teaspoon oregano
⅛ teaspoon cayenne pepper
a pinch each onion and garlic powder

Melt butter in a saucepan and whisk in flour. Cook one minute and whisk in half-and-half and seasonings. Continue to whisk to the boil. Remove from heat.

FIESTA DIP

2 cups pinto beans, freshly
    cooked, no salt or pepper
    added, plus cooking
    liquid as is needed
3 slices of bacon, cooked
    crisp (optional)
1 tablespoon butter
½ cup chopped onion
1½ teaspoons garlic

1 tablespoon chopped
    jalapeño
4 ounces softened cream
    cheese
½ cup sour cream
½ teaspoon salt
½ teaspoon cumin
½ cup grated Monterey Jack
    cheese

Sauté the onion, garlic, and jalapeño briefly in butter. Place in the bowl of a food processor along with remaining ingredients, except bean cooking liquid and cheese. Puree, adding as much bean liquid as is necessary to make a smooth consistency. Spread dip in a casserole dish and sprinkle with grated cheese. Bake in a 400 degree oven until cheese melts and dip is hot. Garnish with freshly diced tomatoes and chopped scallions. Serve immediately with tortilla chips.

Desserts

TODAY'S SPECIALS
Seafood Chowder
Oriental Brown Rice Salad
The Chipotle Choice
Zucchini Pizza

We keep the apple uglies
on top of the case.

BLUE ICING

I was careful, during the months following my mother's death, to sift flour twice before measuring, to avoid stepping on cracks in the sidewalk, and to make sure that all the car doors were securely locked. Though my mother had doubtless tried to teach me other lessons about life, those were the ones I happened to remember. She died three days before Christmas, when I was twelve. The following June when my father, brother and I moved from North Carolina to West Palm Beach, Florida, the cooking chores devolved upon me—the only female member of the family.

I knew how to cook two items: chocolate marble cake and jelly pies. It would make an uplifting, heartwarming story if I could report that I rose to the occasion, as so many fictional heroines have done, and learned to become a marvelous—or even adequate—cook. The fact is, I did not.

Well, I tried. I remember thinking that it would be nice to cook some French fries as a surprise for my father, brother and Joe Getties, a friend from North Carolina who was visiting my brother. We had on hand a can of whole baby potatoes, packed in water. I drained them, cut them in slices, and put them in a pan with a couple of cold sticks of butter. I then turned the heat on high and waited for the potatoes to fry. To my surprise, the kitchen gradually filled with smoke as the butter first melted, then browned, and finally blackened, while the potatoes stayed a sickly shade of white.

My father and brother dutifully ate the fries. My father even managed to wax enthusiastic, though I think he must have been making mental notes to remember *never* to buy canned white potatoes again. Joe, bless his heart, even agreeably tasted a few. I say "Bless his heart," because Joe lived on a strict diet of peanut-butter crackers. He had come to us after hitchhiking clear across the country and back, and he made a point of talking about how well he had lived by eating only peanut-butter crackers. When he arrived at our house, he stocked up on his staples and never touched any other food that I can recall, except my canned whole-baby potatoes.

My mother had left behind a single cookbook which I dutifully perused, but I found the experience perplexing and confounding for two reasons, the first being that the book had been published during World War II when rationing was in effect and the recipes gave all sorts of bizarre substitutes for ingredients that weren't currently available. These were no longer the war years, and I could not figure out how to substitute for the substitutes. The second difficulty was that my mother had once cut her hand rather badly when slicing onions and had bled over about the bottom third of the book. The blood had soaked through most of the pages so that the ingredients—given at the top—were legible, while the directions—given at the bottom—were obscured by dried brown blood.

Using this same World War II cookbook, my mother had taught Claudia Thompson and me to bake a chocolate marble cake. This was in 1953, when my friend Claudia and I were ten years old. For some reason we took it into our heads to enter our chocolate marble cake in the Cleveland County Fair. Every afternoon after school we practiced baking cakes, some days at my house, some days at hers. Mama was patient in going over the steps in baking a proper cake. We sifted the flour twice before measuring, and then once again after measuring with the baking powder and salt. We creamed the butter and sugar until fluffy. We beat well between each addition of egg. We added the flour and milk alternately, beginning and ending with the flour. We greased and floured our pans. After adding the batter to the pans, we tapped the pans twice on the table to remove all the air pockets. We tested the cake for doneness with toothpicks and finger-tips. We cooled the cake thoroughly on racks before frosting.

I don't remember how many layers of cake we baked and froze in Claudia's freezer and mine before we picked what we thought were the three most perfect layers and frosted them with chocolate-marble icing. It seems to me that it must have been a good two dozen.

After frosting our three-layer cake, we put a clear-glass cover over it and proudly delivered our product to the bakery judges at the annual fair.

The Cleveland County Fair, when I was ten, was the biggest thing in the world, larger than the First Baptist Church and the Christmas Parade. Claudia and I moved up and down the long sawdusted aisles of the bakery exhibit, noting with awe that not only were we the only ten-year-olds represented in this competition among Cleveland County's finest bakers, we were apparently the only people under eighteen.

When we came to our cake, which was no longer whole, for the judges had cut a slice to sample, we did not know how to react. There, attached to the glass cover, was a fat red ribbon! We had won second prize for baking at the Cleveland County Fair! The event was simply too big for words. We visited the fair almost daily during its eight-day stay. Daily we paraded past our cake. Mrs. Beam, our fifth-grade teacher, was excited by our red ribbon and elicited from us a promise to share the cake with our class when the fair was over.

Shy but proud, we came to school on the Monday following the fair with our dome-covered cake and set it on a table in front of our class, all of whom wiggled in silent anticipation of the event to come.

What we and Mrs. Beam and our classmates failed to consider were the effects of a dust-covered table, of a sawdust-covered floor, of eight days of October Indian summer heat—the effects of all of this on a cake with a slice cut out of it on the first day of the fair.

In order to share the cake with the entire class, we had to cut small slices, which, for our classmates, turned out to be a blessing. I noticed, when I was slicing, that the chocolate marble frosting bore a curious resemblance to its namesake, marble; and that the texture of the cake itself had undergone a mysterious metamorphosis so that it looked like—even smelled like—sawdust. It tasted like sawdust too. I have never heard such silence as that which descended upon our fifth grade class while we consumed our mercifully meager slices of red-ribbon chocolate-marble cake.

I gave up cake-baking after that, pursuing other interests until we moved to Florida, when I felt duty-bound to cook. I had long since memorized the recipe for yellow cake, and the World War II cookbook contained the chocolate-marble frosting. But I wanted to branch out. Besides, the chocolate-marble frosting had literally left a bad taste in my mouth. There was a single recipe for a basic white frosting that was unobscured by blood, so I decided to try that. It turned out rather well. My father ate nearly the whole cake.

I began to bake the cake on a regular basis, so often, in fact, that I soon began to feel a need for variety. But there were no other legible icings, other than the dreaded chocolate-marble. There was, however, a set of little bottles of food coloring that my father had evidently packed up from my mother's cooking supplies.

I began to experiment. Sometimes I would color the cake; sometimes I colored the frosting. Eventually I colored both. My favorite—the combination I at last settled upon and baked repeatedly—was blue on blue. Blue cake, blue icing. My preference was pale blue for the icing, though I sometimes misjudged and ended up with a vivid electric-blue foam.

Looking back, I wonder if my father was at that time putting in his bid for sainthood. How many times can a person cheerfully consume blue cake with blue icing? Or perhaps it was my blue icing that urged him on in his whirlwind courtship of my soon-to-be stepmother, Letha.

From North Carolina she would write us letters describing what food she happened to be cooking that night. My father and brother and I would sit around our bare table reading her letters aloud, each of us practically tasting her fried chicken and sweet potato pudding and slow-simmered pole beans and angle-flake rolls.

I baked her a single blue-iced cake in welcome, of which she was most appreciative. Then I thankfully let go of recipe books, cake measurements, little bottles of food coloring, and blue icing.

WHOLE WHEAT-PINEAPPLE CARROT CAKE

The Cake
3 eggs
1 cup packed brown sugar
1 cup granulated sugar
1 teaspoon vanilla
1½ cups vegetable oil
2 cups all-purpose flour
1 cup whole wheat flour
1 teaspoon baking soda
2 teaspoons baking powder

2 teaspoons cinnamon
1 teaspoon salt
2 cups grated carrots
1 small can crushed
  pineapple (8½ ounce),
  drained, juice reserved
1 cup raisins
1 cup chopped pecans

Grease a 13 x 9 inch baking pan and line with wax paper. Beat the eggs in an electric mixer. Gradually beat in the sugars, vanilla, and then the oil. Mix together the flours, baking soda, baking powder, cinnamon and salt. Stir flour mixture into the egg mixture to just combine (do not overbeat). Stir in the carrots, pineapple, raisins and pecans. Pour batter into prepared pan and bake in a 350 degree oven until a toothpick comes out clean when inserted in the center (about 45-50 minutes). Cool 5 minutes and invert onto a wire rack. Peel off paper and cool completely. Spread cream cheese frosting over the top and sides.

Cream Cheese Frosting
½ pound cream cheese,
  softened
1½ cups powdered sugar

1 teaspoon vanilla
1 tablespoon pineapple juice

In an electric mixer beat the cream cheese until smooth. Beat in the vanilla, pineapple juice, and powdered sugar. Continue beating until light and fluffy.

CHOCOLATE FUDGE CAKE

The Cake
1 stick butter
½ cup vegetable oil
1 cup water
2 large eggs, beaten
2 cups all-purpose flour
1½ cups sugar

¼ cup cocoa
1 teaspoon cinnamon
1 teaspoon baking soda
½ cup buttermilk
1 teaspoon vanilla

Preheat oven to 350 degrees. Combine the butter, oil and water in a saucepan and heat until the butter is melted. Cool slightly and mix in the beaten eggs. In a large bowl sift together the flour, sugar, cocoa, cinnamon and baking soda. Stir the butter mixture into the dry ingredients along with the buttermilk and vanilla. Grease a 16½ x 11½ inch sheet pan, line it with waxed paper, and grease again. Pour the batter onto the pan and bake until the cake comes away from the sides. Cool for 5 minutes and unmold by turning the pan upside down onto a sheet of plastic wrap. Trim the edges of the cake and spread on the frosting. Using the plastic as a guide, roll up the cake tightly, removing the plastic with each turn, to form a jelly roll. Wrap well in another sheet of plastic and refrigerate for several hours.

Almond Fudge Frosting
1 stick butter, softened
2⅔ cups confectioners sugar
¼ cup cocoa
¼ cup half-and-half
    (approximately)

1 teaspoon vanilla
1 cup chopped, toasted,
    slivered almonds

Cream the butter in an electric mixer. Mix together the sugar and cocoa and beat into the butter. Beat in the vanilla and half-and-half to obtain a spreading consistency. Beat in almonds.

To Serve
Cut the chilled cake into slices and top with whipped cream and a few additional toasted almonds. For an extra rich treat that kids love, spoon chocolate sauce (see recipe page 134) over each slice and then top with whipped cream and toasted almonds.

FRUITCAKE VS. HUMMINGBIRD CAKE

The memories have all run together like so many muddy rivulets into one large North Carolina red-clay stream—all those individual occasions when I sat with my stepmother in some sweetly-smiling, white-haired lady's Christmas-decorated living room staring at a china platter loaded down with thick slabs of dark, damp, deadly-dense, liquor-laced fruit-cake.

"You simply must try my fruitcake," our hostess would inevitably insist, wielding her silver server with all the gentle threat of the most courteous knight. Intent on forcing not merely physical compliance but, more significantly, verbal acquiescence, she politely waited, her polished server flashing in the glow of red and green Christmas tree lights.

"Why, yes, we'd love to," my stepmother would instantly reply. "It looks...delicious," she would invariably add, with no more than a heartbeat's hesitation, she who—excellent baker that she was—had never allowed a fruitcake to pass through her own oven door.

I—a mere adolescent—was allowed a slightly sullen, "Yes, I'd like some, please," but there was clear understanding that I would consume all but the last morsel on my plate.

While those days are more than thirty years in my past, I still find it difficult simply to say when I am offered the inevitable seasonal slice of fruitcake, "No, thank you." Actually, I have managed to say it on a few occasions, but my reply has never been accepted at face value. "Oh, don't you like fruitcake?" is the incredulous, probing response. To which I mumble something like, "I never developed a taste for it," only to be met with the quick, smiling rejoinder, "Well, then, you'll have to taste mine. It's a recipe I've made over the years. I know you'll like it!" Thus I force down a few dense chunks and try to keep smiling.

But no more. Something happened after I turned 50. I realized that people who foist their fruitcake upon me at Christmas time are overbearing and rude and might be cheerfully but firmly denied. After conducting an informal survey among my acquaintances, I realized something further: I'm not the only one who doesn't like fruitcake.

Henry doesn't like it. His primary objection is to all that gummy candied fruit. Fruits in baked goods, however, are a traditional part of holiday cooking, as are nuts. Therefore, for December—and for any celebration—we offer some delicious recipes that make liberal use of uncandied fruits and nuts.

Hummingbird cake is a favorite year-round recipe in many households. Henry's Christmas rendition with its maraschino cherries has a decidedly festive appearance. I've often eaten the three-layered version, but the cake looks more special when baked in a fluted ring or tube pan and it keeps better in this form, too, staying perfectly moist when refrigerated. Also it may be baked ahead of time and frozen, then taken out and frosted at party time. The cream cheese frosting that accompanies the cake recipe is delicious, but for those who like a lighter topping, a glaze may be substituted. The formula for the glaze is 1 tablespoon of melted butter to 1 cup of powdered sugar with 1 to 2 tablespoons of water (or pineapple juice reserved from the can of pineapple used in the cake recipe may be substituted for the water). Simply combine the ingredients and drizzle over the cake, using either fingertips or a spoon.

CHRISTMAS HUMMINGBIRD CAKE

3 cups flour
2 cups sugar
1 teaspoon baking soda
1 teaspoon baking powder
1 teaspoon salt
1 teaspoon cinnamon
⅛ teaspoon allspice
3 eggs, beaten
1 cup vegetable oil

1 teaspoon vanilla
8 ounces crushed pineapple, undrained
2 cups mashed, very ripe bananas
1 cup chopped dates
1 cup maraschino cherries, drained and quartered
1 cup chopped pecans

Sift together the flour, sugar, soda, baking powder, salt, cinnamon and allspice. Combine remaining ingredients and stir into dry ingredients. Pour into a well-greased and floured 10-inch fluted ring or tube pan. Bake at 350 degrees for 1 hour and 10 minutes, loosely covering with foil after 35 minutes. Cool 10 minutes. Invert to remove from pan. Cool completely on wire rack before frosting. Sprinkle 1 cup of additional pecans over the top.

Cream Cheese Frosting
8 tablespoons butter, softened
8 ounces cream cheese

1¾ cups confectioners sugar
½ teaspoon vanilla

In an electric mixer, beat the butter and cream cheese until light and fluffy. Add the sugar gradually until well combined. Beat in vanilla.

HOLIDAY PINEAPPLE UPSIDE-DOWN CAKE

Pineapple upside-down cake is another year-round favorite that attains a festive holiday beauty when maraschino cherries and pecan halves are added. The following recipe was created with the help of Jeannie Cox in our Orange Blossom kitchen. The buttermilk cake itself, without either the fruit or the nuts, is delicious. With the brown-sugar and butter glaze and the topping of pineapple and nuts, the cake becomes a mouth-watering treat. But what makes it a truly heavenly dessert is the addition of rum-whipped cream. A cautionary note for rum lovers: don't be tempted to add extra rum to the whipped cream. The taste will become overpowering rather than seductive.

Fruit and Nut Mixture
1 20-ounce can of pineapple
   chunks, drained
12 maraschino cherries,
   stemmed and drained
½ cup pecan halves
¼ pound butter
⅔ cup brown sugar

The Cake Mixture
2 cups flour
1⅔ cups sugar
2½ teaspoons baking powder
1 teaspoon salt
¼ pound butter, at room
   temperature
1 cup buttermilk
2 teaspoons vanilla
2 tablespoons pineapple
   juice
2 eggs

Preheat oven to 400 degrees. Melt ¼ pound butter in a cast iron skillet. Arrange pineapple, cherries and pecans on top of butter. Sprinkle brown sugar evenly over the fruit and nuts. Sift together flour, sugar, baking powder and salt and place in mixing bowl. Beat in butter and buttermilk and continue beating at high speed until the mixture is smooth. Add eggs, vanilla and pineapple juice. Beat 2 minutes longer. Pour batter into skillet. Place skillet in preheated oven, bake 20 minutes, then cover loosely with aluminum foil and bake 20 minutes more, or until a toothpick inserted comes out clean. Cool 10 minutes. Invert onto a serving dish. Serve warm or cold with rum-whipped cream.

Rum-Whipped Cream
1 cup whipping cream
2 tablespoons sugar
1 tablespoon light rum

In electric mixer beat cream to soft peaks. Add sugar. Beat until firm. Beat in rum.

PIE CRUST

For Two-Crust Pie
2 cups flour
½ teaspoon salt

¾ cup shortening (or
    substitute 10 tablespoons
    chilled butter and 2
    tablespoons shortening
    for a butter crust)
ice water

Combine flour and salt in a food processor and mix together. Cut short-ening into small pieces and add to the flour. Process using on-off turns until flour has the texture of coarse meal. Place mixture in a large bowl and mix in ice water lightly with fingers until dough comes to-gether (about 9-10 tablespoons). Gather dough together and place on a lightly floured surface. Smear dough all over once by pushing with the heel of the hand. Reform dough into a block, dusting lightly with flour. Cut off slightly more than half the dough for the undercrust and wrap it and the remaining piece for the top crust, separately, in plas-tic wrap. Refrigerate for 15 minutes before rolling.

CRANBERRY-APPLE PIE

4-5 cups peeled and thinly
    sliced apples
1 cup cranberries
1 cup sugar

1½ tablespoons cornstarch
¼ teaspoon cinnamon
pie pastry for top and
    bottom crust

Line a greased 9 inch deep dish pie pan with pastry. In a large bowl combine the apples, cranberries, sugar, cornstarch and cinnamon. Spoon mixture into pie shell and cover with remaining pastry. Crimp the edge and cut vents in the top crust. Brush the top lightly with milk and sprinkle with cinnamon and sugar. Place pie in a 400 degree oven on a sheet of aluminum foil to catch the drippings. Bake until golden brown and bubbly (about 40 minutes).

HARLEM

In the late 60's when I was teaching in a Harlem elementary school, I took the subway uptown from the stop near my home on West 11th Street, and then walked several blocks from the subway to the school. On my route was a small grocery store in a dilapidated building. The front windows of the shop always drew my attention, for displayed there were things like whole country hams, barrels of pinto beans, boxes of grits, and whole sweet potato pies. Down in the Village some people had opened a fancy restaurant serving these very items and they called it soul food. To me it was just home-cooking, the everyday fare I'd grown up on. Though I was never tempted to enter the fancy Village soul-food restaurant, I took a few minutes nearly everyday to stop in the Harlem grocery to purchase a couple of thick slabs of ham or stock up on grits; and never, once I had sampled it, did I come away without a healthy slice of nourishing southern-style sweet potato pie. It was custardy and sweet with brown sugar and not overloaded with spice—exactly like the sweet potato pie I was accustomed to eating at home.

This version reminds me of that Harlem sweet potato pie. It contains three eggs rather than two, thereby increasing the custardy texture, and we've tamped down on the spices so that the taste of the sweet potatoes comes through. Keep in mind that a slice of still-warm pie served with vanilla ice cream or a dollop of whipped cream—while not precisely a taste of heaven—is indeed one of earth's genuine delights.

SMOOTH AND SWEET POTATO PIE

2 large fresh sweet potatoes	**1 teaspoon cinnamon**
¼ cup melted butter	**½ teaspoon ginger**
3 eggs, beaten	**¼ teaspoon nutmeg**
1 cup evaporated milk	**¼ teaspoon cloves**
½ cup brown sugar	**dash of salt**
2 tablespoons molasses	**1 cup chopped pecans**
2 tablespoons maple syrup	**(optional)**

Bake the sweet potatoes in a 400 degree oven until soft when pierced with a fork. Peel and puree in a food processor while still hot. Place 1¼ cups of puree in a mixing bowl and beat in the butter. Beat in the eggs and the remaining ingredients. Pour filling into an unbaked pie shell and bake in a 350 degree oven until set (about 50 minutes). If you like pecans with your sweet potatoes, sprinkle over when filling is partially set. Serve with vanilla ice cream or whipped cream.

SCOHARIE CREEK BLACKBERRY PIE

Pastry for Two-Crust Pie
2 cups flour
½ teaspoon salt
10 tablespoons butter,
   chilled

2 tablespoons shortening
ice water

Combine flour and salt in a food processor and mix together. Cut butter into small pieces and add to flour along with shortening. Process using on-off turns until flour has the texture of coarse meal. Place mixture in a large bowl and mix in ice water lightly with fingers until dough comes together and place on a lightly floured surface. Smear dough all over once by pushing with the heel of the hand. Reform dough into a block dusting lightly with flour. Cut off slightly more that half the dough for the undercrust and wrap it and the remaining piece for the top crust, separately, in plastic wrap. Refrigerate for 15 minutes before rolling.

The Filling
4 cups fresh blackberries,
   rinsed and drained
1 cup sugar

¼ cup flour
1 tablespoon lemon juice

In a bowl toss the berries gently with the sugar and flour. Mix in the lemon juice.

Assembly and Baking
On a lightly floured surface, roll the bottom crust into a circle. Lightly flour the top and fold in half and then in half again. Unfold dough into a greased 9 inch pie pan pushing gently with the fingers to fit snugly into the bottom. Drape the dough over the top and trim. Spoon in the blackberry filling. Moisten the edge. Roll out the top crust and place over the top. Crimp the edges together and with a small, sharp knife make four long, deep cuts in the top to allow steam to escape during baking. Bake in a 400 degree oven until the crust is well browned and berry liquid begins to bubble through the steam vents. Cool completely on a wire rack. Serve at room temperature with a dollop of vanilla ice cream.

BLACK BOTTOM PIE

The Crust

1⅔ cups sifted flour
4 teaspoons sugar
⅛ teaspoon salt

5 tablespoons shortening
4 tablespoons butter, chilled
ice water

Sift together flour, sugar and salt. With a pastry blender cut in the shortening and then the butter. Add ice water until dough sticks together. Form into a ball, wrap in plastic and refrigerate for 10 minutes. Roll out dough between sheets of plastic wrap or wax paper and fix into a greased 10 inch pie pan. Crimp or flute the edge, cover with plastic wrap and refrigerate for one hour. Cut dough with a sharp knife into 8 equal slices. Bake in a 450 degree oven until lightly browned (about 15 minutes). Cool on a wire rack.

The Filling

2 eggs, separated
⅛ teaspoon cream of tartar
¾ cup sugar
½ teaspoon cinnamon
4 ounces sweet chocolate,
    melted

warm water
1¼ cups whipping cream
1 ounce sweet chocolate
    (for garnish)

Combine the egg whites and cream of tartar in the bowl of an electric mixer. Beat until soft peaks are formed and continue beating while gradually adding ½ cup of sugar and ¼ teaspoon of cinnamon until egg whites are very stiff and shiny. Spread over crust and bake in a 350 degree oven for 20 minutes. Cool on a wire rack. Stir warm water into the melted chocolate to obtain a smooth and creamy consistency (about 1 tablespoon). Spread a ¼ inch layer of chocolate over the meringue, reserving the rest. Whip the cream with ¼ cup sugar and ¼ teaspoon cinnamon. Spread a thin layer of whipped cream over the chocolate.

Fold the remaining whipped cream into the reserved chocolate and spread over the top. Shred chocolate over the top and refrigerate. Cut into 8 slices.

FROZEN KEY LIME PIE

In the early 1970's we spent a month working at the Inn on Cabbage Key, a small island off the west coast of Florida. Near the Inn was a spot of cleared land where a grove of Key lime trees grew. I often walked there, gathering fallen limes in my apron. Inside the kitchen, Henry would use the limes to make the Inn's only dessert: Frozen Key Lime Pie. There was no air-conditioning to cool a person in that intense south-Florida heat. Customers would sit on the screened porch beneath the shade of the banyan tree and savor the cool taste of fresh Key limes sweetened with condensed milk.

1 can sweetened condensed milk
⅓ cup fresh lime juice

1 tablespoon grated lime rind
3 eggs, separated
graham cracker pie shell

Mix together the condensed milk, lime juice, lime rind and egg yolks. Beat the egg whites until they form *soft* peaks (stiff peaks will not allow for smooth blending). Fold the whites into the condensed milk mixture. Pour into the graham cracker pie shell and bake in a 350 degree oven until just set, approximately 10 to 12 minutes. Cool completely and then freeze. Serve directly from the freezer topped with fresh whipped cream and a slice of lime.

DATE SQUARES

Crust

6 tablespoons butter, room temperature
½ cup brown sugar
¾ cup flour
¼ teaspoon cinnamon

¼ teaspoon salt
¼ teaspoon baking soda
¾ cup oatmeal
¼ cup chopped pecans, reserved for topping

In an electric mixer, cream the butter and sugar. Combine the flour, cinnamon, salt, and baking soda and beat in. Stir in the oatmeal.

Filling

8 ounces whole, pitted dates
½ cup granulated sugar

¾ cup water
juice of ½ lemon

Snip each date into 4 pieces and combine in a saucepan with the remaining ingredients. Bring to the boil, reduce heat, and boil gently until water is absorbed.

Assembly and Baking

Grease an 8 inch square baking pan and press in 1¼ cups of the crust mixture. Spread date filling over the top. Combine pecans with the remaining crust mixture and gently press over the top of the date filling. Bake in a 350 degree oven until golden brown (40-45 minutes). Cut into 16 squares.

TRIPLE C CRUNCH

Triple C Crunch is a combination of cake and candy bar; rich, chewy, non-nourishing, and delicious. The name and the recipe were created several years ago by our son Henry. The recipe has evolved over the years, but it has always contained the three C's: chocolate, caramel, and coconut.

1½ cups Baker's coconut
10 ounces chocolate chips
⅔ cup melted butter
5 ounces evaporated milk

1 package German chocolate
   cake mix
14 ounces caramels
½ cup pecan pieces
1 cup granola cereal

In a saucepan melt the caramels with ¼ cup of the evaporated milk, stirring constantly, until the mixture forms a creamy texture. In a mixing bowl combine the cake mix, butter, and the remaining evaporated milk. Add the pecans. Spread ½ of this mixture in a non-greased 9 x 13 inch baking pan and bake at 350 degrees for 6 minutes. Remove the pan from oven. Pour hot liquid caramel over the top. Sprinkle chocolate chips, coconut, and granola cereal over the caramel. Dab the remaining cake mix over the top, by teaspoonfuls. Bake for 15 minutes. Cool and cut into squares.

GRANOLA

Homemade granola makes a tasty, nutritious breakfast with milk and fresh fruit and is delicious sprinkled over plain yogurt that has been sweetened with honey. In addition, it can be used as a partial substitute for flour in baking recipes for added nutrition and flavor.

1½ cups raw wheat germ
1 cup rolled oats
½ cup wheat bran
2 tablespoons brown sugar
2 tablespoons vegetable oil

½ cup sesame seeds
½ cup sunflower seeds
½-1 cup sliced almonds
raisins

Combine wheat germ, rolled oats, bran, brown sugar, and oil. Spread evenly on a sheet pan and bake at 300 degrees, stirring every 5 minutes, until toasted. Combine sesame and sunflower seeds and toast as above. Bake almonds until lightly browned. Combine everything and add raisins to taste.

CHOCOLATE MINT DREAM

2 large scoops vanilla ice
   cream
2 Oreo cookies

3 Andes mints
3 ounces half-and-half

Place one scoop of vanilla ice cream into a blender. Add 2 Oreo cookies, two Andes mints, 3 ounces of half-and-half and then the second scoop of ice cream. Blend until smooth and pour into a frosted glass. Top with whipped cream and the third mint. For a delicious after-dinner drink, add a jigger of peppermint schnapps before blending.

BUNUELO RELLENO

This is our son Henry's favorite dessert. Henry was born on August 31, 1979 and for his fourteenth birthday he requested just two things: a jet ski ride and a Bunuelo Relleno. As fate would have it, Hurricane Emily arrived the afternoon of August 31st and, though we missed the jet ski ride, we remember well his Bunuelo Relleno that we made with the power out and the wind howling.

The Shell
1½ cups flour
½ teaspoon baking powder
½ teaspoon salt
1½ teaspoons sugar

¼ cup milk
2 tablespoons melted butter
1 egg, lightly beaten

Sift together the dry ingredients. Combine the liquid ingredients. Stir the liquid ingredients into the dry ingredients. Gather the dough together into a ball and knead briefly, until smooth. Divide into 10 equal portions and shape into balls. Let rest, covered, for 10 minutes. Roll each ball into a 4 inch circle and place on a plate lined with plastic wrap and divide each pastry circle on the plate with another sheet of plastic. Just before serving time, deep fry the pastries in 360 degree oil. To form a cup, use an empty vegetable can with the lids removed. Holding the can with a pair of tongs, press it down into the center on the pastry circle. Continue pressing until the pastry is lightly browned and firmly shaped. Remove shells from oil and turn upside down on paper towels to drain. While pastry is still hot, sprinkle over a mixture of cinnamon and sugar.

Chocolate Fudge Sauce
1 stick butter
2 cups sugar
1 cup cocoa

2 cups milk
2 tablespoons cornstarch
½ cup cold water

In a heavy pot, cook the butter and sugar for a few minutes, stirring constantly. Whisk in the cocoa and milk and bring to the boil. Dissolve the cornstarch in cold water and whisk into the boiling liquid. Cook for a few minutes and remove from the heat. Cool and refrigerate.

Final Assembly
Place 2 or 3 scoops of vanilla ice cream into each shell and top with chocolate fudge sauce, whipped cream, toasted slivered almonds and a cherry.

TOM ANGELL'S REFRESHING
PINEAPPLE ICE CREAM

On the day when Tom Angell first began to influence the course of Mehaley Harrow's life, he gathered his eggs as usual early in the morning and arranged them with care in his basket. He then washed his face and hands in fresh cool water and changed into a clean white, long-sleeved shirt and white pressed pants before making his way up the road to Ballance's General Merchandise to exchange his eggs for canned pineapple and condensed milk, ingredients he needed for making his Sunday ice cream. Strolling up the winding sandy lane, he took time to greet whomever he knew to be lonely for news and conversation, but he did not tarry overlong, for he had it in his mind to be at Ballance's with his eggs while they were perfectly fresh. On summer days people were wont to conduct their business in the relative cool of the morning, especially as it had been an unusually hot, dry summer thus far, with a constant, sticky southwest wind heating not only the bodies but also the tempers of those who ventured forth from the shade of their porches. When Tom Angell stepped onto the front stoop of Ballance's Merchandise that morning, at least one temper inside the store was already on the verge of erupting.

In the notions corner, Mrs. Frances Styron was attempting to guide her niece in the selection of a proper color in a hair ribbon to go with her new Sunday dress.

Mehaley Harrow insisted on a wide black velvet band.

Frances Styron had selected pink.

"It ain't fittin' for a 12-year-old miss to go about wearing a black ribbon in the middle of the summer, and velvet at that." Frances Styron's voice could be heard throughout the store as Tom Angell opened the front screen door. Being somewhat hard of hearing, she tended to shout.

Mehaley had lived with her great-aunt for only the past two weeks and had not yet accustomed herself to either Frances Styron's loud voice or her manner of tying up several unrelated ideas in a single sentence and then—without affording her listener any time to disentangle the various threads—sewing in a whole skein of new notions with the next breath.

Such was now the case as Aunt Frances proceeded, her voice rising to new heights.

"I made you a pretty white dress and I even come in here to buy a special pattern to make it by when you don't see me buying a fancy pattern for my own dress, now do you, and here you're settin' up to purchase a black ribbon as if pink was some kind of disease."

She pronounced the last word "*dis*-eze," with the accent on the first syllable. For added emphasis she grabbed a fistful of the skirt of her own dress and shook it. "Pink is a fine color."

As Mehaley's gaze settled on the faded flesh-colored sprigs of some unidentifiable flower on the sagging skirt of her aunt's flour-sack dress,

135

the word "fine" echoed in her mind. Aunt Frances pronounced it with the Banker's brogue, as "foin," just the way Mehaley's mother had always said it.

"Oh, Mehaley and me had a *foin* day in the Park!" she would tell Mehaley's father at the dinner table. Having learned her grammar lessons at one of the more exclusive schools for young ladies in New York City, Mehaley was well aware of the incorrectness of her mother's "Mehaley and me," as well as the provincial ring to her pronunciation of "fine." But oh—how she had always loved to hear her mother speak.

"A fine color for a 12-year-old miss," Frances Styron repeated, and let go of her skirt.

Mehaley's gaze lifted. Her aunt was tall and thin with tightly-curled gunmetal-gray hair, a huge beak of a nose, and astonishing, piercing blue eyes. Meeting those eyes, Mehaley enunciated carefully, "Nonetheless, I prefer the black."

Mehaley's "nonetheless's" and "prefer's" set Frances Styron's teeth on edge. It was highfalutin' talk, learned on the country beyond the sound, and she had no use for it. She was on the point of telling the girl straight out, when out of the corner of her eye she spotted the neat figure of Tom Angell in the doorway.

"Why, Tom Angell!" she called. "He'll tell us the right of it," she added in what she thought was a whisper to her niece. "He's a man of taste and that's a fact. Neat as a pin and keeps a right tidy house. You should see his collection of fine china."

She broke off as Tom Angell eased the screen door shut behind him and acknowledged her greeting with a "Good morning, Miss Frances."

"Come right on over here, Tom, and give us your opinion on these here ribbons," she said, making a wide sweeping motion with her right hand.

"Well, now, Miss Frances, I can't say as how I'm much of an expert on the subject of ribbons." Shifting his egg basket so that he was now gripping it in front of him with both hands, he rocked slowly back and forth from his heels to his toes there in the doorway.

"Course you do," Frances said, dismissing his polite refusal. "A body what knows all about fine china plates can most certainly pick out a quality ribbon. My niece is going to mommick me to death before I get my business concluded. I tell you what's true. I disremember whether you've met her yet?"

"No, Miss Frances, that I haven't."

Shifting his basket again to his right hand, Tom moved toward them, walking with a careful dignity, as was his habit.

Mehaley stared at him. He was colored. She had never been introduced to a colored person. Her grandmother—her father's mother—employed one colored servant in her large brownstone in Washington Square. The rest were Irish. While her mother and father were living, Mehaley had not visited her grandmother's home, for there was some trouble between her mother and grandmother. But she had stayed there for six months after her parents' deaths while her grandmother was determining how best to dispose of her, and during that time she had learned the servants' names. The colored servant was called Betty. She was a cook and stayed in the kitchen. Her grandmother kept her because she could cook anything under the sun and was "a coveted prize," in her grandmother's words, a prize which her grandmother's friends would have liked to have stolen away from her if they could have.

"Mehaley," Frances Styron said, "mind your manners and bid good morning to Tom Angell."

"Good morning," she repeated obediently, looking up at him. His eyes were a deep dark brown, exactly the shade of the imported Dutch chocolates her mama gave her every Christmas.

"This is Bathsheba's daughter, come to live with me," Frances Styron said.

"I can surely see the resemblance between you and your mama," Tom Angell said. "She used to come and visit on Sunday afternoons when she was a girl."

"That's right," Aunt Frances said. "Tom here makes ice cream every summer Sunday. Everybody goes to his house. Lots of young people, lots of socializing, and the best ice cream you'll ever taste."

"Maybe you'll drop by, come Sunday," Tom suggested, his eyes smiling, "and try some of my ice cream."

"I don't care for ice cream," Mehaley said, which was not precisely true. She had once loved ice cream, but that was Before. She divided everything in her life into Before and Now, and she was careful to keep them separated. Not wanting, however, to hurt Tom Angell's feelings, she added, "Thank you all the same."

"Land's sake," her aunt said, "I've never heerd of anybody what didn't like a good bowl of fresh, cold ice cream in the middle of a hot summer day! I'll bring her Sunday, Tom, I surely will, her 'don't care for's' disregardless. And now this ribbon business. You tell her black ain't the color, Tom."

Tom shifted his egg basket from one hand to the other and cleared his throat. "Well," he said, "as for myself, I've always been partial to blue. This one here now with the pretty little cornflowers and the black border." He reached out and touched a length of ribbon. "This one's about as pretty as a body could wish for."

Mehaley's gaze shifted from his face to the ribbon. It was pretty, and it did have a black border. She caught her lower lip between her teeth as she thought about the ribbon and her requirements. Her grandmother had not cared about her black dresses. Aunt Frances, however, did care— for some reason Mehaley couldn't fathom. It was none of her business, after all, what Mehaley chose to wear. Nonetheless, last week she had taken Mehaley's black dresses into the backyard and burned them, leav-

137

ing Mehaley with her two gray dresses and the one white dress which she had thus far refused to wear. Gray was so nearly black that it accorded with her requirements. White certainly did not. But she had decided that a black ribbon with a white dress would be acceptable. Would a blue-flowered ribbon with a black border also do?

"Well?" demanded Aunt Frances.

After a long pause, Mehaley said, "The blue one is acceptable."

Tom Angell nodded. "It's right couthy, that it is," He cleared his throat. "I'd best be gettin' these eggs up to the counter. It's real nice to have met you. You stop by one of these first Sundays and I'll tell you some stories about your mama when she was a girl."

He smiled fondly and shook his head. "That girl was a piece of work, weren't she just, Miss Frances?"

Frances' eyes darted uneasily to Mehaley, who stood stiffly at her side. "That she was, Tom," she said quickly. "Now you go on about your eggs. We do appreciate your help, don't we, Mehaley?"

Her aunt poked her in the ribs. Mehaley said automatically, "Yes. Thank you." Saying the words forced her to let out the breath she had been holding. She did not breathe well whenever anyone mentioned her mother. As she went about the store with her aunt, Mehaley glanced now and then at Tom Angell, so chocolate-brown in his bright white clothes. She watched him take his store book from his rear pocket and place it on the counter for Mr. Ballance, watched him slowly shift his egg basket to and fro over the smooth wooden surface, watched him whoop with surprise as Mr. Ballance's dog Jack leaped onto the counter, heard Tom Angell say, "Near thought I'd die over that surprise, old Jack, near thought I'd die." He rubbed the dog behind the ears. Jack wagged and sat down on the counter to be petted and talked to, looking into Tom Angell's eyes.

Later, when her aunt had purchased all of her "necessaries," as she called them, and Mr. Ballance had recorded them in her store book, she and Mehaley strolled down the windblasted dusty road side by side, Aunt Frances making a running commentary in her loud voice on so-and-so's garden that needed weeding and so-and-so's roof that had leaked since the autumn storm and so-and-so's sagging front porch and so-and-so's tear in her front screen door that had allowed a black snake to slither inside the house a few weeks back.

"Why, I heerd Suzannah Belle clear from my rosebed, I surely did— screaming at the top of her lungs when she woke up from her afternoon nap to find that snake snoozin' on the floor next to her sofa."

Mehaley found it easy most of the time to drift away from her aunt's constant chatter, but occasionally she could not help taking note of what was being said, as was now the case.

"What did she do about the snake?" she asked.

"Do? Why, she didn't do nothin' but jump up and down on her sofa cushions screamin' like an Injun for the first minute or so. I come runnin' from my yard and old Ishmael set out from his house but by the time we got there that Suzannah Belle had done leaped onto the easy chair and scrambled over the back and run off to the kitchen for her broom. She was shooin' that snake towards us when we come bustin' through the front door, which, when we saw what was happenin', of course, we run straight out again."

"And did she get the snake out?"

"She surely did. Screamin' all the while, she was. Screamin' all the while."

Mehaley had been introduced to Suzannah Belle Midgett, a short, round woman with bright pink cheeks, white dimpled hands, and a starched apron. The thought of her jumping over chairbacks and shooing snakes out her front door made Mehaley giggle aloud.

Aunt Frances glanced down at her niece's curly head and nodded, "And did I tell you about the time when old Ishmael's gold that he hid in his mattress got flooded into the road?"....

Stories of neighbors and storms and daily deeds—such was the way her aunt passed the time with Mehaley during the first uneasy weeks of their acquaintance, with Mehaley tuning in and out, in and out. Sometimes she wandered across her aunt's yard. By her grandmother's standards, it was a homely, scraggly place, and the rose garden that Aunt Frances prided herself on could in no way compare with the lush and formal garden kept by her grandmother's gardeners in the rear of the Washington Square brownstone. But her aunt's garden was a comfortable space, all the same, and Mehaley spent what time she could there during the hot summer days.

When Sunday came, she wore the white dress and the blue-flowered, black-bordered ribbon to church and she ate Sunday dinner with her aunt and several relatives in her aunt's dining room. Afterwards the adults sat out on the wide front porch and talked, their voices rising loud and raucous, while Mehaley drifted across the yard in the Sunday afternoon heat. Eventually someone suggested that they stroll over to Tom Angell's for an ice cream, and Aunt Frances called to her to come along.

He lived not far down the road from Aunt Frances in a house which she called "a right noble place." The house was, in fact, more elaborate than most of the homes Mehaley had seen in the village. It had two dormer windows, a large bay window on each side, and an ornate diamond-shaped window under the eaves. Both bay windows were arched, giving the house a churchlike appearance. The lawn surrounding the house was spacious and well-kept. There were swings and stone benches and lawn chairs scattered about. Most of them were occupied by girls and women in their Sunday dresses. Men gathered in little clusters, wearing their good slacks and white shirts.

Aunt Frances, one hand gripping Mehaley's elbow, took her around the yard, introducing her here and there to people she had not yet met.

Mehaley did not have anything to say to these strangers—which seemed not to bother the adults, who would utter a few words and go back to their adult conversations. But the girls she met stared at her, looking her over from head to foot, apparently waiting for her to speak, and when she did not, they turned their backs and ran off to jump rope in a far corner of the yard.

She was standing alone beside some shrubbery and trees when she saw Tom Angell approaching, a dish of ice cream in his hands.

"Thank you all the same, but I told you I don't care for ice cream," she said when he drew near enough to hear her.

He chuckled, "Oh yes, I do recollect you sayin' so. This is for me. I always like to taste what I make, and I saw you standin' over here and hoped you might not mind if I come to pass the time of day while I cool off with some of this pineapple ice cream."

Mehaley did not look at him.

" 'Course if I'm intrudin'...."

Her mama and papa had taught her not to be rude. "You're most welcome to join me," she said, then, hearing the frosty tone of her own words, added hastily, with a quick glance at him, "Truly."

He grinned, "Why, thank you." He took a spoonful of ice cream from his pretty, cut-glass bowl. "You surely have traveled a long ways from New York City to here, a long ways. Your mama, now, she traveled a long ways, too, only in the opposite direction, from here to there."

Mehaley made no comment. Only held her breath and stared straight ahead. "Did she ever tell you how she worried over that distance?" he asked. Mehaley glanced up at him. He was eating his ice cream with slow appreciation.

"I don't know what you mean."

"Why, the distance between here and there," he said, gesturing with his spoon. "Between her home here on Hatteras"—he pronounced it *Ha*-truss, the way her mother did—"and that far-away island, Manhattan, that she was to make her home when she married your papa. She would come here on a Sunday afternoon and her ice cream would just melt away in her bowl unheeded while she worried over making that trip to a far-away island." He took another bite of ice cream. "I recollect it well."

Mehaley looked out over Tom Angell's lawn, taking in the women in their summer dresses, the boys playing tag, the girls skipping rope, the men clustered in little knots.

"But she had my papa," Mehaley said at last. "He was waiting there for her in New York. She told me about that—about how he was wearing a red carnation in his lapel."

"That's true, that's true," he agreed. "That do make a world of difference in traveling a distance, when there's somebody standing by at the end. Most especially wearing a red carnation."

"Yes, it most certainly does," she said, hearing the vehemence in her own voice and wishing she could take back the words. But he did not seem to notice.

"Did anybody tell you how I come to be living here?" he asked, spooning up the last of his ice cream.

She shook her head, surprised at the change of subjects.

"I lived on the country when I was a boy," he said.

Mehaley had by this time heard the expression, "on the country," often enough to know that it meant anywhere on the mainland across the sound. Apparently it could be anywhere from Elizabeth City to New York City. To the islanders, if it was beyond the sound, it was "the country," a foreign land.

"My mama had a deal of children and she gave me up to a couple traveling to Hatteras. Mr. Angell was to be the light station keeper out in the sound. So when I was a boy, I left my mama and my brothers and sisters and come away to Hatteras with the Angells."

Mehaley watched at he removed a neatly folded white handkerchief from his pocket and carefully dabbed at the corners of his mouth, then refolded and replaced the handkerchief in his pocket. "A right long journey it was," he said. Nodding his head slightly, he cleared his throat. "I see Miss Frances comin', and I can tell you what she wants."

Mehaley saw her too, striding purposefully across the lawn. She was wearing her Sunday best, a navy-blue linen dress that matched her piercing blue eyes.

"She wants to make me eat some of your ice cream," she said.

Tom Angell smiled. "No ma'am. She wants me to show you my china collection, so you'd best be prepared to look at some dishes. I declare, you'd think they belonged to Miss Frances herself, she's that proud of them."

Tom Angell was right. Mehaley did not know or care about china or other items which a person might find worthy of collecting, but Aunt Frances loved the fine pieces in Tom Angell's china cabinet and the figurines on the tables and the musical instruments laid out in the living room and the elegant wooden furnishings. All of it had belonged to the Angells, and it was now in Tom Angell's care for the remainder of his life.

When Aunt Frances and Mehaley were leaving, Tom said, "You be sure to come back another Sunday now, Miss Mehaley, and we'll converse."

She did come back, every Sunday for the rest of that summer. She wore her white dress and her blue-flowered, black-bordered ribbon. And they conversed. Tom told her stories about her mother, Bathsheba Styron Harrow, when she was a girl. Mehaley listened, and sometimes she questioned. Gradually she forgot all about holding her breath and took the hot summer air full into her lungs. And she began to tell Tom Angell stories of her own, about living in New York City, about her grandmother's house, even about her grandmother's decision to "dispose" of her in a faraway place called Hatteras.

Sometimes when she and Tom were talking, two or three of the girls would gather round, and then Tom would tell all of them stories about their mamas and papas and everyone would laugh. On a Sunday afternoon near the end of that summer, after one of those stories, one of the girls grabbed Mehaley's hand and pulled her away.

"Come on and jump rope," the girl said. Her name was Cora Beth.

As she skipped across the green lawn with Cora Beth, Mehaley glanced back over her shoulder at the neat figure of Tom Angell. He was smiling, nodding his head, eating a dish of pineapple ice cream.

When it was Mehaley's turn to jump, she felt all the heat of the late summer day pumping in her veins as she exerted her legs to lift from the earth in rhythm with the turning rope. With the girls calling encouragement, she was able to keep up the pace for quite a while. When the rope inevitably tripped her up, she was ready for a breather. Her mouth felt dry, her throat parched.

"Come on," said Cora Beth. "Let's get us some ice cream."

As the two girls headed toward the ice cream table, Tom Angell spotted Mehaley Harrow's blue-flowered, black-bordered ribbon lying forgotten in the grass near the spot where it had come undone while Mehaley was jumping rope. Later, when everyone had gone home for the night, he would retrieve it for her and take it inside his house to keep with all his treasures, in case she should ever need it further.

Meanwhile, knowing it to be her preference, he dished up a bowlful of chocolate ice cream for Cora Beth. For Mehaley he prepared a bowl of his own favorite: rich and creamy and refreshing pineapple ice cream.

Thomas Vine Angell grew up, lived, and died in Hatteras village after being brought to the island as a boy by Inez and Nelson Angell when Nelson Angell became the keeper of the Oliver's Reef Lighthouse in 1874. The marker on Tom Angell's grave in Hatteras village indicates he was born in 1864 and died in 1937.

He made pineapple and chocolate ice cream and served it on weekends at his home.

"Tom Angell's Refreshing Pineapple Ice Cream" is a work of fiction, and all of the incidents in the story except for one are entirely fictional. The exception involves Mr. Ballance's dog Jack who did, in fact, surprise Tom Angell one day in Ballance's General Merchandise as he was bringing in his eggs. Many thanks to Clarisse Ballance Gray for relating to me her memories of Tom Angell and her father's store.

The story is dedicated with love to all of those on this island and "on the country beyond the sound" who have experienced the loss of people they cherish and who have had the courage to travel distances in their hearts in order to find the refreshment life can afford.

REFRESHING PINEAPPLE ICE CREAM

Years ago Tom Angell, a kindly man and the island's only black resident, would invite neighbors in Hatteras to his home on Sunday afternoons during the hot summer months for conversation and homemade pineapple ice cream. After talking with several older people on the island, we created this recipe to approximate the custard that Tom Angell might have used.

Vanilla Custard

2 cups milk	**¼ cup cornstarch**
2 cups half-and-half	**1 tablespoon vanilla**
4 eggs	**1 can sweetened condensed**
1 cup sugar	**milk**

Scald milk and half-and-half. Mix together the sugar and cornstarch. In an electric mixer, beat the eggs well. Continue beating while gradually adding the sugar and cornstarch. Slowly beat in the hot milk and half-and-half. Pour into a heavy saucepan and cook, whisking constantly, almost to the boil (180 degrees). Remove from the heat and stir in the condensed milk. Cool to room temperature and stir in the vanilla.

Final Preparation

2 cups fresh or canned	**vanilla custard**
crushed pineapple, well	
drained and finely chopped	

Add the pineapple to the custard and refrigerate until very cold. Freeze in an ice cream maker.

BUXTON WITHIN

The Vermonter was middle-aged and plump-looking in his multiple layers of serviceable faded wool. While filling his gas tank, he gazed ruminatively at the stickers affixed in random order to the rear window and bumper of our salt-corroded, dented Trooper, parked on the opposite side of the island of pumps from his Chevrolet.

I got out of the Trooper and tried without success to zip up my new goosedown-lined jacket. As I tugged and yanked, the Vermonter hummed a little ditty and rocked gently back on his booted heels, his gaze drifting back and forth from the entertaining array of stickers to my apparently equally entertaining efforts to master my zipper.

"Say now," he began in an easy, conversational way, his eyes crinkling at the corners, "would Buxton be a school?" With a nod of his head, he indicated the sticker on our bumper which read, "Where in the Hell is Buxton?"

I glanced up at him—wondering what in the world had given him the idea that Buxton was a school. "No. It's a town," I replied curtly, giving another tug at my zipper.

"Ah!" he said, as if suddenly enlightened. "A town, you say." He rocked back on his heels and studied our mud-splattered license plate. "In North Carolina?" He shifted his position to replace the gas nozzle in its holder.

I glanced up at him again. He was smiling in a genial, inoffensive manner. Feeling somewhat chagrined at the thought of my former abruptness, I took the time to explain to him that Buxton was a small town on the Outer Banks of North Carolina.

"They have some weather down there," he observed.

"Yes," I agreed, wrapping my arms around my waist. "You have some weather here, too. My blood's too thin for this cold."

"Well," he said, "I suppose that's true. But we don't have hurricanes. Just snow and thick heads."

By this time Henry had finished paying the attendant and obtaining directions for our next destination. I gave a final tug at my zipper. It worked.

"You drive carefully," he said, turning toward his Chevrolet. "And watch out for those hurricanes down there in Buxton."

"The Vermonter at the gas station thought Buxton was a school," I told Henry a few minutes later when we were underway.

"*What* the Hell *is* Buxton, anyway?" he asked with a smile.

Thinking of our island home as I looked out the window at a pristine, crystal Vermont winter day, I added, "And *where* is it right now?"

Our Buxton bumper sticker had held an appeal for us from the first time we saw it four years ago at Buxton Under The Sun, a shop located next door to our bakery in Buxton.

We had never intended to live in Buxton, our assumption being that if we ever moved to the Outer Banks, we would naturally live in our summer cottage in the poetic-sounding village of Hatteras. But circumstances led us with an astonishing inevitability to the whimsically individualistic heart of "downtown" Buxton.

Whenever we told any of our acquaintances back in Chapel Hill that we were moving to plain, prosaic-sounding Buxton, they inevitably asked, "Where's that?"

"On Hatteras Island, near the Lighthouse," we would explain.

"Oh, yeah. Hatteras. Beautiful place. Lots of storms," was the standard reply.

No one off the Outer Banks seemed to have the least clue as to where Buxton was. Thus the appeal of the bumper sticker. We did not buy one, however, for while I was perfectly willing to ride around advertising such profundities as "Cuddle Up With a Cat," "The Best Defense is Self-Defense," "If you Must Drink and Drive, Drink Pepsi," and "J'ai Traverse le Trou Canadien En Planche A voile!", I drew the line at displaying a profanity on my Trooper.

We sailed through our first Buxton storms after our move: Hurricane Bob, the Halloween Storm, the March 1993 N'or Easter. If it was inconvenient to be without power and to be cut off from the Upper Banks, it was also exhilarating to feel the force of Nature without directly experiencing any material loss other than revenue.

By the time Emily was forming in late August of 1993, I felt like an old pro at handling storms. The entire experience of getting ready for her arrival was uncannily reminiscent of the final day of my pregnancy. I washed my hair and all of our clothes. I vacuumed and mopped. I was ready.

But Henry was feeling wary. "I don't know about this storm," he said. "I have this feeling."

Henry gets these "feelings" sometimes. And they are, I've learned, to be respected. So when he said, "Maybe we should leave," I listened.

"But what if we can't get back?" I pointed out. "The road will probably wash out at Pea Island—maybe even right here in Buxton at the motels."

"Well, what could we do here anyway if we stayed?" Henry reasoned.

"But this is my home!" I blurted out, feeling somewhat surprised at my own words, for I had been in Buxton fewer than three years at that time, while I had lived in Chapel Hill nearly fifteen. Yet I had never particularly thought of Chapel Hill as home. It was just the place where I happened to be spending my days and nights. "I don't want to leave," I said. "We might not be able to get back."

So we waited. Early on the morning of August 31, Henry said, "The roads are still clear. Everybody else who's going has already left. It's an easy drive if we go now."

Heretofore I had considered myself to be a person who was amenable to reason. Henry's proposal was eminently reasonable: everything secured—an easy drive with no traffic—a vacation—electricity—air-conditioning—all the amenities. Yet inside of me there was this stubborn lump of resistance. The closer Emily drew, the bigger the lump grew.

"I can't leave," I admitted at last.

"Okay," he said. "I think I'll go stock up on beer."

Our son Henry, whose fourteenth birthday fell on August 31, had listened to our debate. "It's okay with me," he said, "as long as we can still fix bunuelos." Bunuelo Relleno is a Mexican treat composed of a deep-fried flour tortilla filled with vanilla ice cream. "And one other thing," he added. "I'd like to buy that bumper sticker from Buxton Under The Sun and put it on the Trooper."

Suddenly it seemed like a suitable thing to do.

As our son affixed the bumper sticker reading "Where in The Hell Is Buxton?" to the rear window of the Trooper, Henry and I watched. "You know," he said, I saw another sticker on a car recently that answered this question."

"What did it say?" I asked. "We should get that one, too."

"I can't remember."

He shrugged and went inside to fix bunuelos while the winds began to howl.

Throughout that afternoon and evening of the hurricane he tried to remember what the other bumper sticker said. "It was something zen-like," he mused, sitting in a rocking chair and sipping his beer while we looked out our apartment window at the liveoak tree being stripped of its leaves by the speaking wind.

Sitting in our rockers in front of our window, we played a truncated version of Trivial Pursuit. As the minutes and hours ticked by, we grew euphoric.

"This isn't so bad," I said. "I think Bob was worse."

"Let's go out on the porch and take a look," Henry suggested around 7:00 that evening.

The wind and rain were still driving hard but we were able to make it out onto our porch. It was unnaturally dark for the hour.

"What's that in the road?" I asked, pointing to Highway 12.

"A river," Henry the younger replied.

We stared in awe at the water flowing down the road.

"Oh my God," I said, following with my eye the path of water as it flowed to the left and down into the newly formed lake which hours before had been the parking lot of EMS and Centura Bank. There was an abandoned EMS ambulance, its emergency lights still flashing, floating in the center of the lake.

We stayed on the porch for half-an-hour, then returned to our apartment to wait out the night. I couldn't sleep. I kept picturing the river of water in the road and the ambulance tilted at a crazy angle in the temporary lake. We had been fortunate. I knew we had been fortunate. But I could not help thinking about the water in the road and the people who lived up the road and down the road, and I could not sleep.

Around 3:30 AM when it was completely calm, I decided to take the dog out for a walk. Henry joined me. The night was warm. The still air was laden with the scent of pine. I inhaled repeatedly and deeply. Never before had I smelled anything so fresh and new as that scent of pine.

"Look at the moon," Henry said, his voice the only sound in the silent night.

Over the bakery the moon was a brilliant white in an utterly clear midnight-black sky. It was almost too bright to look at—as if it were the sun.

After a while, we headed back inside, side by side.

"I remember what the other sticker was," Henry said as we picked our way through the debris.

I looked over at him. "What?"

He smiled. "Buxton is Within."

For a year and four months after Emily, I didn't really understand. I still refused to leave the Outer Banks. It was as if I feared that if I left, Buxton would somehow disappear.

But as we drove away from the Vermonter at the gas station and up into the clean white mountains in early January, 1995, I thought of Buxton and Emily, of the scent of pine, of the brilliance of the white moon and of ambulances floating in a storm-made lake, and it suddenly struck me that Buxton, after all, was that zen-like thing, a state of mind; and that even when I left for awhile, I actually did carry it within.

147

Rainbow's End
in
Buxton

INDEX

V

W

Z

Night Lights
in
Burton

~NOTES~

$\sim$*NOTES*$\sim$

~ *NOTES* ~